W9-CFZ-122

SLAVES, PEASANTS AND CAPITALISTS
IN SOUTHERN ANGOLA 1840–1926

AFRICAN STUDIES SERIES

Editorial board

John Dunn, Lecturer in Political Science and Fellow of King's College,
Cambridge

J. M. Lonsdale, Lecturer in History and Fellow of Trinity College,
Cambridge

D. M. G. Newbery, Lecturer in Economics and Fellow of Churchill College,
Cambridge

A. F. Robertson, Director of the African Studies Centre and Fellow of
Darwin College, Cambridge

The African Studies Series is a collection of monographs and general studies
which reflect the interdisciplinary interests of the African Studies Centre at
Cambridge. Volumes to date have combined historical, anthropological,
economic, political and other perspectives. Each contribution has assumed
that such broad approaches can contribute much to our understanding of
Africa, and that this may in turn be of advantage to specific disciplines.

BOOKS IN THIS SERIES

Slaves, peasants and capitalists in southern Angola 1840–1926

W. G. CLARENCE-SMITH

LECTURER IN POLITICS, UNIVERSITY OF YORK

CAMBRIDGE UNIVERSITY PRESS

CAMBRIDGE

LONDON · NEW YORK · MELBOURNE

DT
611.7
.C5
1979

Published by the Syndics of the Cambridge University Press
The Pitt Building, Trumpington Street, Cambridge CB2 1RP
Bentley House, 200 Euston Road, London NW1 2DB
32 East 57th Street, New York, NY 10022, USA
296 Beaconsfield Parade, Middle Park, Melbourne 3206, Australia

© Cambridge University Press 1979

First published 1979

Printed in Great Britain by
Western Printing Services Ltd, Bristol

Library of Congress Cataloguing in Publication Data
Clarence-Smith, W. G.   1948–
Slaves, peasants and capitalists in southern Angola
1840–1926.
(African studies series; 27)
Bibliography: p.
Includes index.
1. Angola – History – 1648–1885.   2. Angola – History –
1885–1961.   3. Angola – Economic conditions.   4. Angola –
Social conditions.   I. Title.   II. Series.
DT611.7.C5   967'.302   78–67805
ISBN 0 521 22406 3

Contents

Illustrations

Preface

A great deal has been written about southern Angola between 1840 and 1926, but almost always within the framework of a narrow colonialist historiography. Portuguese writers of the Salazarist era presented a picture of their colonies which was ordered around the process of *portugalização*, an ugly neologism which can be translated as 'portuguesification'. This process was further broken down into three broad phases: discovery, conquest and assimilation. Southern Angola was associated with the feats of the nineteenth-century Portuguese explorers of central Africa, and the area was particularly famous as the scene of the exploits of the military heroes of the late nineteenth and early twentieth centuries, whose names still adorn so many of the streets and squares of Portuguese towns. The development of a deeply-rooted white settler community and the evangelizing efforts of catholic missionaries were also used as illustrations of the assimilationist theme and as foundations for the hopes of a new Brazil. The publications of Ralph Delgado, Gastão Sousa Dias and Alfredo de Albuquerque Felner are probably the best and most painstaking examples of this kind of historiography.

A first attempt at writing a quite different history of southern Angola was made in my doctoral thesis, which was presented to the University of London in 1975 under the title 'Mossamedes and its hinterland, 1875–1915'. The present book is based on this thesis, but the two texts differ very substantially. The thesis put forward detailed research findings in a set of chronologically ordered chapters. Portuguese colonial policy provided the main integrating theme, and there was no systematic theoretical interpretation of the material. The problems of resistance and collaboration on the part of African societies assumed a prominent place, in spite of expressed dissatisfaction as to the utility of such concepts. In brief, the thesis did little more than elaborate a general history of the area, with a much greater stress on African societies than was the rule in colonialist historiography.

Preface

The present book has been entirely rewritten. Chapters are divided thematically, and descriptive narrative has been cut down very substantially. Portuguese colonial policy is treated separately in a short chapter, and the main emphasis is laid on the economic and social structures of local social formations. The time-span covered by the thesis has been roughly doubled in order to analyse the whole process of colonial conquest. The epilogue has also been expanded and ameliorated so as to give an outline of more recent developments. Considerable additional research has been carried out in the secondary literature to this end.

From the theoretical point of view, I have relied heavily on recent marxist writings, not only in the historical field but also in the social sciences. I have tried to analyse Portuguese colonial policy in terms of the classes and fractions of classes which struggled to control the state apparatus, and I hope to develop this theme considerably in future publications. A class analysis is made of the local colonial society in southern Angola, and I have attempted to employ the concepts developed by the French school of marxist anthropology in order to grasp developments in African peasant societies. In short, I have used a number of recently elaborated theoretical concepts to make a concrete analysis of a concrete situation.

The sources consulted were entirely of an archival or published nature. I made no attempt to collect oral traditions, partly because I had difficulties in obtaining a visa for a sufficient length of time and partly because of growing doubts as to the value of oral traditions for the historian. This latter problem is discussed in my recent article in *History in Africa*,[1] and further details on archives may be found in my thesis. Here, it is sufficient to say that the major archival and library collections for this study consisted of the administrative archives in Lisbon and Luanda, mission archives in Paris, the newspapers held in the Câmara Municipal de Moçâmedes, and the libraries of the British Museum, the School of Oriental and African Studies, the Sociedade de Geografia de Lisboa and the University of Zambia (concentrated stacks). Additional archival research since the thesis was completed was carried out in the National Archives of Zambia, the Manuscript Collection of the Livingstone Museum, the Pretoria archives and the Public Record Office.

Both primary and secondary sources for this area are plentiful. Indeed, they are considerably more abundant than the poverty and small population of the area would seem to warrant. This is due to the fact that southern Angola was a sensitive frontier area which proved difficult to conquer, and also to the presence of white settlers and missionaries from an early period. Southern Angola has been fortunate as well in the treat-

[1] Clarence-Smith, 1977a.

viii

ment it has received at the hands of scholars of other disciplines, notably ethnographers and geographers.

I would like to end by expressing my thanks to all those who helped me in the writing of thesis and book. The Department of Education and Science made the whole project financially viable and was very generous with travel grants. The School of Oriental and African Studies and the University of London (Central Research Funds) made appreciable extra grants for maintenance and travel respectively. Professor Roland Oliver supervised the writing of the thesis with patient care and made many valuable suggestions. Dr David Birmingham originally proposed the topic and helped me with many points of detail, as well as guiding me through the archives of Luanda. Professor Joseph Miller, Professor Franz-Wilhelm Heimer, Dr René Pélisser, Father António Brásio and the late Father Charles Estermann all made available to me the fruits of their detailed knowledge of Angolan affairs. Father Bernard Noël opened the archives of the Holy Ghost Fathers to me and gave me much of his precious time. I would also like to thank the innumerable people who helped me in one way or another and who are too numerous to mention. However, particular thanks are due to Jill and Alberto Dias, René Naville, Margaret and John Davis, Frank Hollis, Victor Jorge, Nuno Ferreira, Renato Mascarenhas, Jorge de Figueiredo, Ian Frazer, Richard Moorsom, Roger Wagner and Sue Newton-King. Finally, I owe an especial debt of gratitude to my sister, Annette Elliot, who typed the original thesis version with infinite patience.

Note on proper names

Geographical names are spelt according to standard local cartographic usage (e.g. Caconda not Kakonda). In cases where more than one name is current, the most commonly used form in English has been adopted (e.g. Okavango not Cubango). Modern Portuguese orthography has been used throughout (e.g. Moçâmedes not Mossamedes). Where names have been changed, the form current during the period under consideration is retained (e.g. South West Africa not Namibia).

Names of African peoples are spelt according to standard international Bantu usage (e.g. Cokwe and not Chokwe or Tshokwe). Plural prefixes for African names are not employed (e.g. Kwanyama not Ovakwanyama), except in a few cases where it has become established usage to do so (e.g. Ovambo).

Note on currency

Portuguese currency has been converted into pounds sterling throughout, in order to avoid the problems posed by the fluctuations of Portuguese currency and in order to facilitate comparisons with the southern African region as a whole. The smallest unit of currency was the *real*, plural *reis*. In 1910, a new unit was introduced, the *escudo*, worth 1,000 *reis*. Statistics were often expressed in *contos*, an accounting unit worth 1,000,000 *reis* or 1,000 *escudos*.

Before 1861, the so-called weak *reis* were used in Angola, the value of which was slowly falling in relation to the metropolitan *reis*. In the 1850s, there were about 7,000 weak *reis* to the pound. From 1861 to 1891, metropolitan *reis* were used, with a fixed official parity of 4,500 *reis* to the pound, although actual exchange rates were often more favourable to the pound. After 1891, Portugal was effectively off the gold standard, and the exchange rate until 1919 fluctuated between 4,500 *reis* and 8,000 *reis*. This was followed by a period of hyperinflation, so that in 1924 there were 127,500 *reis* to the pound, although this had dropped again to 95,000 by 1926. A further complication is introduced by the fact that the pound itself fell rapidly in terms of its purchasing power between 1914 and 1920, and then rose again slowly during the 1920s. Moreover, there existed a separate Angolan *escudo* in the 1920s, worth only about 80% of the metropolitan *escudo*. An almost complete set of exchange rates were obtained for the period after 1891, but figures for the years before 1861 are very scarce. For precise references, see the list of sources.

In view of these complications and of the doubtful reliability of many statistics, all figures should be taken as no more than rough approximations. Figures have been rounded up or down in order to remove all illusion of precision.

Abbreviations

AGCSSp	Archives Générales de la Congrégation du Saint-Esprit
AHA	Arquivo Histórico de Angola (Av: Avulsos; Cod: Códices)
AHM	Arquivo Histórico Militar (P: Pasta)
AHMH	Arquivo Histórico do Museu da Huíla
AHU	Arquivo Histórico Ultramarino (R: Repartição; P: Pasta)
AMAE	Archives du Ministère des Affaires Etrangères (CP: Correspondance Politique; NS: Nouvelle Série)
AS	*Annual Series*
BG	*Bulletin Général*
BO	*Boletim Oficial*
C de M	*Correio de Mossamedes*
CG	Curador Geral
DGU	Direcção Geral do Ultramar
FO	Foreign Office
GB	Governador de Benguela
GG	Governador Geral
GH	Governador da Huíla
GM	Governador de Moçâmedes
J de M	*Jornal de Mossamedes*
NAZ	National Archives of Zambia
P em A	*Portugal em Africa*
PRO	Public Record Office
TRP	Très Révérend Père

Introduction

Although this book is primarily a case study of a limited area and period, it must also be placed briefly in the context of two influential schools of historiography current in the 1960s, which can be labelled 'African nationalist' and 'uneconomic imperialist'. The 'African nationalist' school has provided a view of the colonial epoch which makes the imposition and eventual withdrawal of European rule the fundamental points of historical reference. African resistance or collaboration then form archetypal social processes, which subsume all others. These responses are further subdivided according to the categories of modern or traditional and élite or mass.

Such an approach has been rejected as unsatisfactory, because the concepts employed are imprecise in the extreme, and because the absolute predominance of the political level is simply assumed. African and European are effectively racial categories, and traditional and modern are distinguished according to the vague criterion of the assimilation of western cultural features. As for the terms élite and masses, they rarely mean any more than the few and the many. At no point does one get a clear analysis of the economic interests of different classes and fractions of classes, of the political means which such groups adopt in order to further their perceived interests, and of the ideological constructs which underpin political and economic struggles.

In this case study, an attempt is therefore made to grasp the social processes in the colonial epoch more clearly by making a class analysis. A primary distinction is drawn between a local colonial social formation, which was characterized by the dominance of capitalist relations of production, and a cluster of tributary peasant social formations, in which pre-capitalist relations of production continued to predominate. The class structure of colonial society is analysed in chapters 3 and 4, while the resistance to class formation in peasant societies is the major theme of chapters 5 and 6. At the same time, the nature and evolution of the

1

unequal relationship between an expanding colonial nucleus and dominated peasant societies are kept constantly in mind. In this way, it is hoped that a number of neglected or controversial issues have been placed in a clearer perspective.

One of the most neglected but currently controversial issues facing independent Angola is that of the development of a true proletariat. Vague terms such as 'working class' evade the crucial issue of the extent to which labourers have become divorced from the means of production. In this study, it is argued that a proletariat developed very precociously in parts of southern Angola, as a result of the effective maintenance of quasi-slavery until 1913. Slaves were uprooted from their communities of origin, lost all rights in peasant societies, and became totally dependent on wage labour in the colonial nucleus when they were freed. But as soon as a more normal African pattern of recurrent migrant labour was established, this particular process of proletarianization was halted. A much more diffuse and slow form of proletarianization ensued, the rate and intensity of which was dependent on the capacity of African peasant societies to continue ensuring the reproduction of the labour force outside capitalist relations of production. In simpler terms, the rate and level of proletarianization depended on the relative importance which wages assumed for the subsistence of peasants and their families. The early stages of this process are examined in chapters 5 and 6, in conjunction with the growth and decline of petty commodity production for the market. In the epilogue, two examples are given of peasant societies which had reached an advanced level of proletarianization by the 1970s.

A second problem which still generates much controversy concerns the nature and roots of ethnic and racial antagonisms within central colonial societies. In this study, it is suggested that such antagonisms sprang largely from the economic insecurity of petty bourgeois elements in colonial society, who were constantly threatened with proletarianization and struggling to break out of a vicious circle of debt. Racial and ethnic factors were thus used by sectors of the petty bourgeoisie to increase their own security at the expense of others. An attempt is therefore made to distinguish as clearly as possible the different fractions within this highly complex and varied class. It is further argued that the racism of the local capitalist class was of a different origin, being principally concerned with control of the labour force and the forging of political alliances with certain sectors of the petty bourgeoisie.

Thirdly, the vexed problem of the nature of pre-capitalist or non-capitalist relations of production in peasant societies is examined. A model of a lineage mode of production is sketched out, which stresses the communal ownership of the means of production, the apportioning of

2

labour power according to kinship, the relatively egalitarian redistribution of surplus product and the low level of development of the forces of production. It is argued that the central historical process within such societies is not the class struggle as such, for constituted classes do not exist, but rather the attempt by certain groups to turn themselves into an exploitative class, and the resistance to such a process by other groups. On balance, it is suggested that resistance to class formation was very effective, even in as extreme a case as the Ovambo, who at first sight seem to provide an example of a transition to feudal relations of production. With the generalization of colonial rule, the resistance to class formation was generally buttressed by colonial policies which aimed at securing a satisfactory flow of cheap migrant labour.

The second influential school of historiography which has been rejected in writing this book is that which contends that Portuguese colonialism in the nineteenth and early twentieth centuries was not economically motivated. According to this school, Portugal was an underdeveloped and backward nation, which inherited colonial possessions in Africa by historical accident and set out to expand them for reasons of humiliated national pride, in spite of the fact that these colonies were a constant and heavy burden on the finances of an already poor country. The explanation for this phenomenon is held to be that the Portuguese ruling class was seeking a rather indistinct set of social, political and ideological gratifications, which are subsumed under the general category of 'Veblenian conspicuous consumption'.

Southern Angola would appear to provide a classic illustration of the theory of uneconomic imperialism. The budgetary deficits of the region were consistently the largest in the colony, often turning a positive balance into a negative one. The natural poverty of the region and the effective military resistance of its peoples to colonial conquest meant that millions of pounds were spent for no apparent reward. At the same time, the foreign-owned chartered Companhia de Moçâmedes proved a resounding economic failure. This study is not centrally concerned with these problems, but they are considered briefly in chapter 2 and they are essential to the general context of the book. A number of objections to the theory of uneconomic imperialism are therefore set out below.

The first objection is really a very simple point of logic, namely that the lack of economic returns in no way suffices to prove a lack of economic motivations. Colonies were seen by all European powers in the nineteenth century as speculative long-term investments, which might not provide any immediate profits and which might indeed never provide any profits at all. In southern Angola, the Portuguese government genuinely believed that the Cassinga gold mines could turn out to be a 'second Rand',

3

thus compensating manyfold for the initial losses incurred in conquering the region. Similarly, the Portuguese appeared for a brief moment to have found their eldorado during the ephemeral whaling boom of the 1910s.

A more important point is that public deficits must be carefully distinguished from private profits. The state did not incarnate some disembodied national interest, but was the subject of intense conflict between classes and fractions of classes. The powerful groups with strong interests in colonial expansion are briefly examined in chapter 2. To be sure, these groups also paid some of the taxes which were used to pay colonial deficits, but taxes came mainly from other groups and classes. In more general terms, recent research in the field of Portuguese history indicates that the intensification of capitalist relations of production as a whole in Portugal in the late nineteenth century owed a great deal to the existence of protected colonial markets. Southern Angola provided markets for Portuguese textiles, wines and other goods, was included in the sphere of operations of monopolies in the fields of banking and communications, and produced cheap cotton, hides and other raw materials for metropolitan industries. Another minor point, which is easily forgotten, is that many ecclesiastical and military cadres made fine careers owing to their 'heroic' exploits in southern Angola, including some of the individuals who were involved in the military coup of 1926, which put Salazar in power.

Of more central relevance to the present study is the fact that a vigorous group of local colonial capitalists developed, who were crucially concerned with influence over the state apparatus and who have too often been forgotten by the theorists of uneconomic imperialism. In southern Angola, local entrepreneurs depended on the state in the vital question of labour, firstly for the maintenance of quasi-slavery to 1913 and then for the extraction of cheap labour from peasant societies by taxation and forced labour. Commercial capitalists, to the extent that these were distinct from entrepreneurs, needed the state to guarantee security in the interior, to invest in communications infrastructures and to enforce a system of exchange which maximized their profits. The local capitalist class of southern Angola was able to exert substantial political influence in Lisbon – but this is a subject which would require considerably more research.

In a broader perspective, it is hoped that the conceptual framework adopted for this study will prove useful for understanding some of the present problems of the People's Republic of Angola and of other African countries which are attempting social transformations inspired by marxism. In particular, the approach taken in this book underlines the complexities and difficulties inherent in the task of socialist construction. Like other African states, Angola is still far from constituting a single homogeneous social formation, and the problems of transition to socialism are qualitatively different in the central ex-colonial society as compared to the tributary peasant societies. Furthermore, the problem of the structure of exploitation of peasant societies by the central society does not disappear with independence, and it needs to be adequately conceptualized to be resolved. Finally, the central society which has been taken over by the independent Angolan government is still very weak, limited and dependent on the core areas of the capitalist world.

1

Land and peoples

Southern Angola is a somewhat vague geographical term, which is defined for the purposes of this book as the region within the hinterland of the town of Moçâmedes. The concept of hinterland is used in a wide and flexible manner to include all the areas over which Moçâmedes exercised significant influence as a port and administrative centre during the period under consideration, This corresponds roughly to the present provinces of Moçâmedes, Huíla, Cunene and Cuando–Cubango, to which should be added the southern part of Moxico province and the Ovambo and Okavango territories in northern South West Africa.

Southern Angola is an area with few natural or human resources. The land consists mainly of the northern marches of two deserts, the coastal Namib desert and the Kalahari, which are separated by the great African escarpment. Extensive cattle rearing is the major economic activity, and fairly rich fishing is also provided by the cold current along the barren coast. Crop production is limited to a few favoured areas and is more for subsistence purposes than for marketing. There are iron mines at Cassinga, but these were only brought into production during the 1960s. Transport and communications are rendered difficult by the barrier of the escarpment, which is particularly steep to the east of Moçâmedes, and by the vast stretches of arid sandy land. However, there are three excellent natural harbours along the coast, and communications have improved dramatically since the 1950s, with the extension and widening of the Moçâmedes railway, the building of tarred roads and the development of air transport.[1]

The population is small and unevenly distributed. In 1960, there were only just over one million people in the whole area, including northern South West Africa. Vast arid spaces contrast with thickly populated little islands of human activity, which are in some cases subjected to severe problems of overpopulation. Soils are everywhere poor, so that the crucial

[1] Kuder, 1971.

factor limiting human settlement is the availability of water. The distribution of rivers and of highlands with better rainfall thus determines the patterns of settlement, which can be seen as falling into a number of population clusters.[2] In between these clusters there live roving bands of Khoi or Twa hunter–gatherers, who have been of little or no historical importance.[3]

The coastal population cluster, made up of a number of fishing ports and oases scattered along the coast, is the smallest in terms of population, but it is also one of the most economically developed, attracting large amounts of migrant labour. Fishing is by far the most important economic activity, including the processing of fish catches, and this region accounts for about two-thirds of Angola's total production of fish. In 1960, the population of the coastal cluster numbered some 40,000, of whom about 8,000 lived in the town of Moçâmedes. This town is important not only for fishing but as a centre of communications, commerce, administration, tourism and market gardening. The climate of this region is cool and temperate for most of the year, and this has facilitated the growth of a white settler population, which numbered some 7,000 in 1960.[4]

The majority of the population of the coastal cluster are Kimbari, or more strictly Mbali, who are the descendants of the slaves imported into the region in the nineteenth century. They speak a modified form of Ki-Mbundu, the language of Luanda and its hinterland, and their culture is a syncretic mixture of Portuguese and Mbundu elements. They are essentially integrated into European forms of social and political organization, and have no recognizable form of tribal organization. From their base in the coastal zone, the Kimbari have spread inland to towns and other centres of economic activity. In the Salazarist era, many of them were *assimilados*, that is full Portuguese citizens.[5]

About 150 kilometres to the east of Moçâmedes lies a small isolated stretch of land over 1,500 metres in height, known as the Huíla highlands. Rainfall is more abundant than in the surrounding semi-arid areas, permitting the establishment of a denser population. Temporary streams drain the highlands in various directions, so that settlement extends beyond the confines of the highlands. Cattle, maize, cotton and tobacco form the major resources of this region, which had a population of some 150,000 in 1960. About a tenth of the population lived in the town of Sá da Bandeira, recently given back its old name of Lubango, and about the same proportion of the population were whites. Lubango has slowly

[2] Angola, 1964, I; Wellington, 1967; Kuder, 1971.
[3] Estermann, 1976, part I; Guerreiro, 1968.
[4] Kuder, 1971; Marques, 1964–1965, I, pp. 395–426; see map 5, p. 209.
[5] Estermann, 1939; Cardoso, 1966.

become the chief commercial and administrative centre in southern Angola, usurping the position once held by Moçâmedes. Lubango is also the centre for the processing of meat and cereals, and is important in the spheres of communications, tourism and market gardening.[6]

The majority of the indigenous population of the highlands cluster are Nyaneka, who depend in roughly equal proportions on cattle and maize. In the more arid lands to the south and below the escarpment to the west, the Herero ethnic group predominates, characterized by a much greater dependence on cattle rearing. The Nyaneka are divided into a number of small chieftaincies, the most important of which are those of Huíla, Njau and Ngambwe, which also used to rule their Herero neighbours. The origins of the chiefly dynasties, and possibly of chiefly institutions themselves, appear to lie in the complex movements of population and institutional changes which affected northern and central Angola in the sixteenth and seventeenth centuries, and which have traditionally gone under the misnomer of the Jaga invasions. However, very little can be said about the early history of the Nyaneka, given the present state of research.[7]

About 250 kilometres south-east of Lubango, after a desolate stretch of arid thornveld, one reaches a series of flood plains which lie along the frontier with South West Africa. This region had a population of about 450,000 in 1960, of whom over half lived to the south of the frontier. The flood plains of the middle Cunene and Okavango rivers account for under a quarter of this total, and the great mass of the population inhabit the Ovambo plain. This flat sandy plain is flooded by the Cuvelai and other small streams, which run only in the rainy season. The flood waters filter through the Ovambo plain in an intricate maze of broad shallow channels, with some surplus water occasionally draining into the Etosha Pan. The sandy soil is infertile and both rainfall and floods are highly irregular, so that crop cultivation is limited to hardy and drought-resistant millet for subsistence purposes. Fishing is a very important subsidiary source of food, and hunting used to be of great significance. Deposits of iron ore, copper ore and salt used to be the basis for vigorous local trade and artisanal production. However, it is cattle raising which dominates the economy of the region, both for subsistence and for sale. Pastures are generally abundant and of high quality, so that the limit on cattle raising is the lack of water in the dry season.[8]

Population pressure on scarce and limited resources is great in this

[6] Medeiros, 1976; Urquhart, 1963; Angola, 1964, I; Chapman, 1971; see map 6, p. 110.
[7] Estermann, 1956–1961, II and III; Lang and Tastevin, 1937; Miller 1973.
[8] Urquhart, 1963; Neto, 1963; Carvalho and Silva, 1973; Angola, 1964, I; Lehmann, 1954; Wellington, 1967; see map 7, p. 111.

9

region, which is the most deeply and structurally affected by migrant labour in consequence. Unlike other regions of southern Angola, migrant labour is increasingly the result of a shortfall in subsistence production rather than of administrative measures. The flow of labour goes mainly to the mines and fisheries of South West Africa, but it is also of great importance to the fisheries of southern Angola. There are no towns to speak of in the region itself, and no industries, although commercial cattle ranching did develop on the western fringes of the region from the 1950s. The Ovambo and other peoples of the flood plains are thus forced to migrate over long distances to supplement the insufficient subsistence production of their homes.[9]

All the peoples of the flood plains are closely related to the Nyaneka in linguistic and cultural terms. They were probably all affected by the so-called Jaga invasions, although the early history of the flood plains is even more obscure than that of the highlands. Five chieftaincies have been of especial historical importance, the Kwanyama and Mbadya of northern Ovamboland, the Nkhumbi of Humbe on the Cunene bend, and the Kwambi and Ndonga of southern Ovamboland. Together, they constitute the great majority of the population of the region, and the Kwanyama have always been the largest indigenous political unit in southern Angola since the nineteenth century.[10]

The coast, the Huíla highlands and the flood plains make up the core of the hinterland of Moçâmedes, but two other regions should also briefly be considered. The Caconda highlands and south-eastern Angola lay in the hinterland of Benguela in the nineteenth and early twentieth century, but they were both of some importance to southern Angola as a whole. Furthermore, recent administrative changes and developments in communications have integrated these two areas more fully into southern Angola.

The Caconda highlands lie to the north-east of the Huíla highlands, and are more populated and better watered. The population numbered some 260,000 souls in 1960. Sisal, cotton, tobacco and coffee are grown as cash crops on a fairly important scale, in addition to the usual highland staples of maize and cattle. The indigenous inhabitants form part of the great Ovimbundu ethnic group of central Angola, although the Hanya peoples below the escarpment have many cultural links with their Nyaneka neighbours to the south.[11]

The vast sandy plains of south-eastern Angola, excluding the flood plain of the middle Okavango, contained only some 200,000 people in

[9] Moorsom, 1977; Mendes, 1958.
[10] Estermann, 1955–1961, I and II; Loeb, 1962; Urquhart, 1963.
[11] Kuder, 1971; Hauenstein, 1967; Childs, 1969; Angola, 1964, I.

10

1960. This population is concentrated along the courses of the great rivers which flow from the central highlands, and is more numerous in the northerly reaches of these rivers. Cattle raising is little developed for lack of suitable pastures, and there are no cash crops. After the collapse of the wild rubber boom in the 1910s, wax and wood became the only commercial resources of the region, albeit on a small scale. The development of the Cassinga iron mines on the western fringes of the region has had only a limited impact, owing to the highly mechanized nature of mining activities.[12] The Ngangela in south-central areas and the Wiko in the south-east proper share many cultural and linguistic traits and are often referred to under the collective name of Ngangela.[13] Interspersed among them are small groups of Cokwe immigrants from central-eastern Angola, who began to enter the region during the nineteenth century.[14]

In general terms, it is worth stressing once again that southern Angola is a poor area, with a small scattered population and very few natural resources. There is a great body of Portuguese colonial literature which presents the area as a land flowing with milk and honey. This is the result of the history of white settlement. Many officials or private individuals tried to put pressure on the state to stimulate white settlement or to provide services for existing white settlers. Alternatively, colonial propagandists attempted to persuade independent settlers to come out to southern Angola. This gave rise to a very tendentious set of reports and publications, which pictured the south as a new eldorado and exaggerated its economic potential out of all recognition.[15] It is therefore essential to insist on the fact that the south is the cinderella region of Angola, comparable in many ways to the northern territories of Kenya.

[12] Kuder, 1971; Borchert, 1963; Angola, 1964, I.
[13] Pearson, 1970, p. 5; McCulloch, 1951; Schachtzabel, 1923.
[14] Delachaux, 1948; Miller, 1970.
[15] For example, Almeida, 1912, pp. 102–109; Roçadas, 1908, pp. 38–41.

2

The colonial context

Although the main focus of this book is on the social and economic structures at the local level, it is necessary to begin by considering the external constraints within which local societies functioned. This is all the more important in view of the fact that the initiative throughout the period lay with outside forces, and in particular the colonial ministry in Lisbon. Local social formations were far from powerless, but in the last instance they had to bow to the dictates of Lisbon. Colonial policy was in turn shaped mainly by the Portuguese bourgeoisie, which consolidated and entrenched its hold over the state apparatus as a result of the civil wars of the early nineteenth century.[1] The overall trends in colonial policy reflected the changing interests of the bourgeoisie, which became increasingly involved in the colonies as a result of the growing contradictions emanating from Portugal's bourgeois revolution.[2]

Before the 1880s, the African colonies were seen mainly as a source of revenue, which was needed to contribute to the great effort of intrastructural equipment which Portugal was engaged in. The idea of using colonial revenues to develop the metropolis had long roots in Portuguese history, and had been promoted most successfully by the Marquis of Pombal in the eighteenth century.[3] However, after the final loss of Brazil in 1825, the possibilities of using the African colonies to the same end were much more doubtful, and only convinced colonialist politicians such as the Marquis of Sá da Bandeira devoted much energy to this strategy. Sá da Bandeira's tactics were based mainly on increasing customs revenue by stimulating trade and expanding Portuguese control along the coasts of Africa. Less important were efforts to tax African peasants and to develop a local plantation sector with white settlers.[4]

[1] Cabral, 1977; Marques, 1973.
[2] Capela, 1975, chapters 6 to 9; Cabral, 1977, pp. 42–43.
[3] Cabral, 1977, pp. 14–16, 28–29.
[4] Sideri, 1970, pp. 180–181; Wheeler, 1967, pp. 2–4.

12

From the late 1870s onwards the extraction of revenue from the colonies was increasingly overshadowed by a more pressing need for colonial markets.[5] After an initial period of import substitution, Portuguese industry began to be burdened with unsaleable surplus production, especially in the northern textile industry centred on Oporto, and the colonies appeared as the best solution to surplus realization problems.[6] This was rendered more urgent by the crisis in the world economy at the turn of the century, known to contemporaries as the 'Great Depression', which led to cut-throat competition for markets and increasing protectionism, including the famous 'Scramble for Africa'. Portugal therefore vigorously pressed its claims to territory in the African continent and adopted extremely protectionist tariffs in 1892.[7]

For many years, Portugal was content merely to stake out a trading preserve. African peasants were allowed more or less complete autonomy in petty commodity production, and the plantation sector was undeveloped and still worked with slave labour. The major aims of the authorities were to keep trade flowing and to find cheap ways of asserting effective occupation in order to counter any threats of territorial annexations by other powers.[8] This was sufficient to meet the requirements of the textile manufacturers of Oporto.[9] Portugal was still a large-scale importer of capital, and there was little or no metropolitan capital available for investment abroad.[10] As for foreign capitalists wishing to invest in the colonies, they were often treated with suspicion, as the Trojan horses of ambitious colonial rivals.[11] Metropolitan and foreign capital was thus only slowly attracted to the colonies, going first to wealthier areas such as São Tomé and southern Mozambique.[12]

After the republican revolution of 1910, the state took more positive measures throughout the empire to encourage a plantation sector based on migrant labour and to regulate the petty commodity production of African peasants.[13] This involved the prior military conquest of all African societies and the general imposition of taxation and forced labour, measures which had already been successfully adopted since the 1890s by the 'new imperialists' in southern Mozambique.[14] The republic maintained protectionism in general terms, although the tariff policies of the new régime hesitated between the need to afford protection to metropolitan industries and the imperatives of the growth of colonial eco-

---

[5] Cabral, 1977, pp. 42–43.   [6] Capela, 1975, chapter 9.
[7] Munro, 1976, chapter 3; Capela, 1975, chapters 6 to 9.
[8] Couceiro, 1910.   [9] Pimentel, 1903.
[10] Sideri, 1970, pp. 161–164.   [11] Papagno, 1972, pp. 146, 150.
[12] Marques, 1973, pp. 155–157, 159–161.
[13] Marques, 1973, pp. 243–244; Capela, 1977, pp. 15–17.
[14] Capela, 1977, pp. 15–17; Duffy, 1962, chapter 5.

nomies.[15] Republican governments also became increasingly interested in importing colonial raw materials, especially cotton for the textile industry, in order to save on foreign exchange.[16] The period of the first republic was one of great governmental instability and somewhat erratic innovations, but in most ways it prefigured the more systematic policies of the Salazar era, with their emphasis on the exploitation of cheap African labour and an autarkic colonial pact.[17]

Southern Angola only became incorporated into the Portuguese colonial empire from the 1840s, so that the history of the region faithfully reflects the policies of the era of bourgeois predominance, with few or no survivals from earlier periods of Portuguese colonialism. To be sure, Diogo Cão and Bartolomeu Dias had both visited the shores of southern Angola in the 1480s, but they were only concerned with the sea route to India, and during the sixteenth century the caravels steered well clear of the desolate Namib coastal desert.[18] Parts of southern Angola were also included in the trading and raiding hinterland of Benguela after 1617, and in the late eighteenth century there were plans to colonize the southern highlands with white settlers. But in general terms, the Portuguese presence in the south before the 1840s was limited to a handful of obscure slave traders.[19]

The sudden intensification of Portuguese activity in southern Angola from 1840 was due to the crisis consequent on the abolition of the Atlantic slave trade. For a time, the remote ports of the south were used to continue the clandestine export of slaves.[20] But much more important were the attempts to use the south in the general strategy of increasing the revenues of Angola by legitimate means. As elsewhere in Angola, this involved the setting up of customs posts, the taxation of Africans and the stimulation of a plantation sector. However, the emphasis on this latter tactic was greater than in other parts of the colony.

The Portuguese were successful in extending their fiscal control southwards along the coast of Angola, but they did not derive as much profit from this as had been expected. The town of Moçâmedes was founded in 1840 with the main purpose of controlling the growing ivory trade from the interior, which had developed after the abolition of the royal monopoly on ivory in 1834.[21] But Moçâmedes never really prospered as a trading post, mainly because of problems of communication with the

15 Teixeira, 1934, pp. 354, 364, 370.
16 Teixeira, 1934, pp. 362, 695; Marvaud, 1912, pp. 223–224.
17 Wheeler and Pélissier, 1971, chapters 5 and 6.
18 Axelson, 1973.   19 Delgado, 1944, passim.
20 PRO, FO 63–1113, Jackson to Clarendon 29/1/1856; Tams, 1969, I, p. 97.
21 Delgado, 1940, pp. 111–112, 119; Delgado, 1944, II, pp. 26–28.

14

interior, so that Benguela continued to dominate the trade of the south.[22] In the early 1860s, the governor general of Angola complained that the trade of Moçâmedes was insignificant and that the deficits of the settlement were intolerable.[23] Indeed, it was the commercial unimportance of the area which accounted for the fact that the Portuguese did not meet with any foreign resistance to the extension of their fiscal control, unlike the very different situation which arose in the north.[24]

The second way in which the Portuguese government attempted to extract revenue from the south was by conquering and taxing the peoples of the interior, a policy which was briefly put into effect in the 1850s and 1860s. The Portuguese forces reached Humbe on the Cunene, exacted taxes from the Nyaneka and the Nkhumbi, and contemplated the conquest of Ovamboland.[25] But the cost of these campaigns was far greater than the meagre revenue which they generated, and trade was disrupted by the constant warfare.[26] Interior expansion was thus abandoned in the late 1860s.[27]

The stimulation of a plantation sector by state-aided white settlement schemes proved to be the most effective tactic adopted by the Portuguese to raise revenue. In 1849 and 1850, some 300 Portuguese nationals fleeing from xenophobic persecution in Brazil were transported by the state to the coastal oases of southern Angola.[28] The settlers were given lands, seeds, tools and slaves by the government, and measures were taken to ensure that their products could be sold.[29] After difficult early years, the settlers prospered during the cotton boom of the 1860s, and state-aided colonization was successfully extended to the foothills of the escarpment.[30] However, attempts to settle about 200 whites in the Huíla highlands in the late 1850s proved an expensive failure, for communications with Moçâmedes were very poor and lucrative tropical crops were destroyed by frosts.[31] But in general terms, the revenue which Moçâmedes did produce came mostly from the activities of the white settlers who had been brought to southern Angola at the initiative and cost of the government.[32] By the 1870s, the deficits of Moçâmedes had not been eliminated but they had become much less severe.[33]

However, the expenditure and deficits of the south soared once again during the period of the 'Scramble for Africa'. Southern Angola was not

[22] Silva, 1971–1973, 33, p. 254.   [23] Menezes, 1867, pp. 17–18.
[24] Wheeler and Pélissier, 1971, pp. 52–56.
[25] Pélissier, 1975, I, pp. 172–194.   [26] Menezes, 1867, pp. 70–71.
[27] Pélissier, 1975, I, pp. 190–194.   [28] Torres, 1950.
[29] Torres, 1950; Alves, 1970, pp. 141–142 for tariffs to protect rum production.
[30] Torres, 1952.   [31] Delgado, 1944, II, p. 105.
[32] AHU, 1R–Diversos 1868–1888, GM, Relatório 19/6/1877.
[33] AHU, 1R–Diversos 1868–1888, GM, Relatório 19/6/1877.

a particularly attractive area in itself, but it was vital to the Portuguese ambitions of occupying the central African regions lying between Angola and Mozambique. The first threat to these ambitions came from rumours of German plans in the mid-1880s to link their eastern and south-western protectorates at Portugal's expense.[34] The Portuguese therefore sent state-aided white settlers to the Huíla highlands in 1884 to 1886, and built forts among the Nkhumbi and Ngangela peoples in 1883 and 1886 respectively.[35] In late 1886, a compromise was reached, delimiting the frontier as it now stands. Portugal gave up its claims to the 18th parallel as the southern frontier of Angola, in return for a 'free hand' in central Africa.[36] However, the German menace continued to hang over southern Angola to the First World War, fed by plans for Anglo-German partition of the Portuguese colonies and various frontier incidents.[37]

The Portuguese met with a more formidable opponent to their central African dreams in the person of Cecil Rhodes, with his plans for a British empire stretching from the Cape to Cairo.[38] In late 1889, an expedition was therefore sent from Benguela to occupy Barotseland and link up with Serpa Pinto's forces coming from Mozambique.[39] But the Portuguese were forced to call off these expeditions as a result of the British ultimatum in early 1890. The first version of the subsequent Anglo-Portuguese treaty divided Barotseland between the two powers, but Rhodes protested vehemently and managed to have the whole of Barotseland included in the British sphere of influence.[40] The definition of the western frontiers of Barotseland gave rise to exceedingly complex disputes, which were only resolved by arbitration in 1905.[41]

After the British ultimatum of 1890, the Portuguese did their best to reduce the vast deficits of southern Angola, which were mainly responsible for the financial problems of the whole colony.[42] This task was rendered all the more urgent by the severe financial crisis which afflicted the Portuguese government in the 1890s and early 1900s.[43] The Portuguese therefore attempted to maintain effective occupation in the face of lingering foreign threats, while cutting administrative and military costs to an absolute minimum.[44] A wide degree of autonomy was thus granted to three different groups in the interior – settlers, missionaries and chartered

[34] Paiva, 1938, I, p. 110.　　　　　　　[35] Delgado, 1944, passim.
[36] Hammond, 1966, pp. 103–106.
[37] Hammond, 1966, p. 253; Wheeler and Pélissier, 1971, p. 75.
[38] Axelson, 1967.　　　　　　[39] AHU, 1R-1OP, GG to Minister 5/1/1890.
[40] Hammond, 1966, pp. 123, 138, 140 and 146; Axelson, 1967, pp. 250–252.
[41] Pélissier, 1975, I, pp. 551–553.
[42] AHU, 2R-15P, GG to Minister 8/10/1891.
[43] Marvaud, 1912, pp. 82–83.
[44] AHU, 1R-13P, GG to Minister 26/8/1893.

companies – on condition that they upheld the overall sovereign rights of Portugal in the region.

In the Huíla and Caconda highlands, white settlers were given considerable *de facto* powers within the formal apparatus of government. A Portuguese official who had married into one of the leading settler families was made 'Intendant of White Colonization', a new post created especially for the situation. The intendant was expected to maintain order with settler forces, thus minimizing military expenditure.[45] However, this arrangement did not prove very successful, for the Portuguese government was rapidly drawn into the area again by disputes between different settler factions and by complaints as to the treatment of Africans by settlers. The intendancy was thus allowed to lapse after 1900.[46]

Further inland, the catholic missionaries of the mainly French Holy Ghost Fathers order were given subsidies and allowed a wide measure of autonomy. In return. they were expected systematically to occupy the empty spaces of eastern and south-eastern Angola with Portuguese mission stations.[47] Practical difficulties made it impossible for the missionaries to found stations in the vast sandy plains of the south-east,[48] but they did occupy the Ngangela area, where they set up small theocracies under Portuguese protection.[49] The catholic missionaries also rendered notable diplomatic services in Ovamboland, where they acted as official representatives of the Portuguese government in boundary disputes with the Germans.[50]

A number of charters were issued to different groups of foreign capitalists in southern Angola, but only the charter of the Companhia de Moçâmedes was ratified by parliament.[51] The concession of this company, granted in 1894, covered a long and mainly barren stretch of land right along the southern frontier of Angola. The coastal strip was excluded, as were the highlands and the main rubber-producing areas. Nor did the company obtain the right to administer customs posts or tax the African population, unlike the 'majestic' companies of Mozambique, so that it could not simply live off existing revenues.[52] Much of the inhabited area of the concession was also occupied by the warlike and independent

---

[45] AHU, 2R–17P, Minister to GG 20/4/1892; AHU, 2R–23P, GG to Minister 13/8/1892; Paiva, 1938, passim.

[46] AHU, 1R–15P, GG to Minister 15/1/1895 and 30/8/1895; Paiva, 1938, passim.

[47] AHU, 1R–14P, Antunes, Relatório 1/12/1894, in Bishop to Minister 7/12/1894; Brásio, 1966–1971, IV, passim.

[48] AGCSSp, 476–B–I, Lecomte to TRP 15/8/1893.

[49] See chapter 6, pp. 89–93.

[50] For example, AGCSSp, 467–B–II, Lecomte to Rooney 17/7/1901.

[51] Papagno, 1972, pp. 164–166; AMAE, CP–241, d'Ormesson to Hanotaux 13/10/1895; AMAE, NS–Portugal–7, Rouvier to Delcassé 22/4/1899.

[52] Guilmin, 1895; official documents in *BO*, 21/4/1894 and 23/6/1894.

peoples of the flood plains, who were outside any effective control by the company.[53]

The Companhia de Moçâmedes thus had only two strategies for making any profit, mining and railway construction. The Cassinga area was rumoured to have vast gold deposits, and it was hoped that a railway to Cassinga could also serve the Otavi–Tsumeb copper mines in northern South West Africa, and might even be linked up with the Rhodesian railway system.[54] However, the original French concession holders were obscure speculators without the necessary capital for such ventures,[55] so that financial control over the company rapidly fell into the hands of Cecil Rhodes and his associates.[56]

But Rhodes' speculative ventures in southern Angola came to nothing. The Cassinga gold mines did not prove susceptible to large-scale operations, and the company lost heavily in its attempts to exploit the mines.[57] Then German interests prevailed on the German government to build the railway to the Otavi–Tsumeb mines from the artificial port of Swakopmund in South West Africa.[58] The German government also objected to any transcontinental railway line which did not pass through South West Africa,[59] although it was Robert Williams who finally outflanked Rhodes to the north by building the Benguela railway.[60] The Companhia de Moçâmedes was thus reduced by the early 1900s to a small foreign concern, with minor interests in commerce, cattle ranching, cotton and salt.[61] The original concession of the company was finally revoked in 1923, and the company came to specialize entirely in cattle ranching.[62]

Within the area preserved for Portugal by one means or another, the government took the necessary steps to protect Portuguese commercial interests. The differential import duties established by the 1892 tariffs were very successful in replacing foreign textiles by metropolitan textiles on the Angolan market.[63] Various other Portuguese manufactures, such as gunpowder and alcohol, were similarly protected.[64] However, the government was not able to prevent extensive smuggling from neighbouring colonies. In the early 1900s, a representative of the textile firms of Oporto

[53] AHU, Companhia de Moçâmedes – 9, Chefe Humbe to GM 5/1/1896.
[54] Guilmin, 1895, pp. 320–322; Drechsler, 1962, pp. 61–65.
[55] AMAE, CP–243, Minister to d'Ormesson 26/7/1896; *P em A*, 9, September 1894, p. 304.
[56] Drechsler, 1962, p. 59.   [57] Forté, 1931, pp. 13–15.
[58] Drechsler, 1962, pp. 73–74.
[59] Rhodes Papers, C22–24, Jones to Rhodes 2/9/1899 and subsequent documents.
[60] Katzenellenbogen, 1973, pp. 37–43, 47, 64.
[61] AHU, Companhia de Moçâmedes – 10, DGU 26/11/1901; Negreiros, 1907, pp. 282–283; Almeida, 1912, p. 334.
[62] Matos, 1926, pp. 288–290; Forté, 1931, p. 23.
[63] Carvalho, 1900, pp. 90–91.   [64] Carvalho, 1900, passim; Coutinho, 1910.

complained that German cloth was penetrating deep into southern Angola and that the authorities were doing nothing to prevent this.[65] But the German and British governments also complained of illegal smuggling by Portuguese traders of firearms and alcohol into their territories.[66] In a more general perspective, some colonial officials argued that the 1892 tariffs were stifling the overall volume of Angolan trade and were encouraging inefficiency in metropolitan industries.[67]

The influences of the 'new imperialism' began to be felt in southern Angola during the 1900s, and became decisive after the republican revolution of 1910. The state resumed its preponderant role, waging long and expensive campaigns against African peasant societies.[68] This was followed by the imposition of taxation and forced labour throughout the region.[69] Southern Angola was turned into a vast labour reserve for plantations, fisheries and public works.[70] Migrant labour also went on an increasing scale to neighbouring territories, especially South West Africa.[71] The Portuguese disapproved of this loss of labour to other colonial economies, but it was difficult to prevent and it brought in foreign exchange. Migrant labour abroad was thus usually illegal but tolerated.[72] At the same time, peasant production was not actively discouraged,[73] and there remained a minority of rich cattle owners who met their tax and labour obligations through their cattle-raising activities.[74]

The conflict between the plantation and the peasant sectors formed the most basic historical process at the local level in southern Angola during the whole period under consideration. Colonial society, or the colonial nucleus,[75] was a creation of outside forces, but it rapidly developed a dynamic of its own. A vigorous group of local capitalists sprang up, whose interests were sometimes radically opposed to those of metropolitan or foreign capitalists. However, the colonial nucleus was never strong enough to break away from the metropolis, so that the settler leaders followed a policy of lobbying the colonial state in the pursuance of their own interests. In particular, the settlers attempted to use state power to assert the predominance of the colonial nucleus over African societies, in order to extract commodities and labour power from African societies

[65] Pimentel, 1903, pp. 86–87.
[66] AHA, Av–41–71–4, German Ambassador to Minister of Foreign Affairs 16/5/1895; NAZ, KDE 8/1/1, Annual Report, Magistrate Barotse District, 1906–1907.
[67] AHU, 2R–21P, GG to Minister 28/9/1895; Couceiro, 1910, p. 182.
[68] Pélissier, 1975, I, pp. 632–716. [69] Couceiro, 1910, pp. 222–223.
[70] Diniz, 1914, p. 73. [71] Galvão, 1930, p. 237.
[72] Galvão, 1930, p. 237. [73] Galvão, 1930, pp. 156–157.
[74] Rates, 1929, pp. 96–97; Statham, 1922, pp. 152–153.
[75] Heimer, 1976, pp. 49–50.

in the most advantageous manner. The following two chapters are thus devoted to an examination of colonial society, looking first at economic structures and then at the corresponding social and political characteristics.

African peasant societies, or tributary societies,[76] were originally autonomous social formations, but they were slowly subjugated and placed in a position of subordination to the colonial nucleus. This occurred in the first place through a process of exchange, which became increasingly necessary for African societies but the terms of which were controlled by the colonial nucleus. More important was the second stage, in which the colonial state intervened by force, imposing taxation and forced labour. However, African tributary societies were not dissolved nor absorbed into the colonial nucleus, although individuals did become assimilated into colonial society. For reasons which still require more theoretical investigation, the colonial nucleus remained a restricted social phenomenon. African peasant societies were allowed to retain their own social structures, on condition that they provided the requisite cheap labour power and cheap commodities to the colonial nucleus.[77] Chapters 5 and 6 thus examine these developments in African peasant societies.

[76] Heimer, 1976, pp. 49–50.
[77] Wolpe, 1974, for a theoretical analysis of the South African case.

3

The economy of the colonial nucleus

Three phases may be distinguished in the geographical expansion of the colonial nucleus in southern Angola, on the basis of the three general criteria of the private ownership of the means of production, the employment of slave or wage labour and the predominance of production for the market. Between the 1840s and the 1860s, the ports and oases of the coastal strip were brought into production, and in the 1880s parts of the highlands were incorporated into the colonial nucleus. Finally, a few limited areas along the middle Cunene valley were annexed from the 1900s. The colonial nucleus was thus extremely restricted and discontinuous, as could be expected in a semi-arid environment with few resources.

The fishing industry formed an important branch of production from the outset in southern Angola, and from the 1880s onwards it completely dominated the economy of the colonial nucleus. The staple product of the fisheries during this period was dried and salted fish, and Moçâmedes regularly accounted for over 95% of Angola's exports of this commodity. However, the place of fish within Angola's overall exports was always modest, fluctuating between 1 and 5%.[1]

The technology employed in fishing was both primitive and relatively static. Tiny sailing and rowing boats were used for catching the fish, and motorized boats did not appear till the 1930s. Lines and rudimentary nets were commonly used right through the period, although larger nets were employed more frequently from the 1890s. Trawling remained forbidden right into the 1940s. The fish were also badly prepared. The heads were often not removed and the salting processes left much to be desired. But the worst problem was that drying was done in the open and the finished product was thus covered with particles of sand. Over half the dried fish was exported in large sailing boats, which specialized in the Congo estuary trade. These boats would return laden with wood, a precious commodity in the southern desert, and with contraband goods

[1] Azevedo, 1945, p. 143.

21

bought in the Congo Free Trade Zone. Some dried fish was also taken to the island colony of São Tomé in sailing boats, but it seems to have been more normal to use the regular steamers of the Empreza Nacional de Navegação for this route.[2]

The development of the fishing industry was a somewhat uneven process, characterized by booms and slumps. During the 1850s and 1860s there was a modest development of exports of fish oil to the USA and Brazil, but the quality of this product was low, and by the 1870s exports had practically ceased.[3] However, the market for dried fish expanded rapidly from the 1880s, owing to the development of cocoa plantations in São Tomé. The plantation owners found that dried fish from Angola was the cheapest way of providing the necessary protein in the diet of their labourers.[4] São Tomé thus became the main market for the southern fisheries, taking on average 47% of Moçâmedes' exports between 1905 and 1921. The other important market was the Congo estuary, which took 42% of exports over the same period.[5]

But expansion came to a halt at the turn of the century. The value of annual exports, which had risen steadily from about £4,000 in the late 1870s to reach a peak of nearly £40,000 by 1903, stagnated and declined after that date. In 1915, the value of exports reached their lowest point at just over £20,000.[6] The slump was due to overproduction and loss of markets, which led in turn to a fall in prices of about 50% in the late 1890s.[7] Foreign markets were closed to Angolan dried fish, on the grounds that the quality was too poor.[8] And even on the protected Portuguese colonial market, competition from the fisheries of the Cape Verde Islands posed severe problems.[9] In the early 1900s, thousands of kilos of unsaleable rotten fish thus had to be thrown into the sea.[10]

The solution to the crisis lay partly in the improvement and diversification of production, which began to get under way during and after the First World War. Drying operations were increasingly carried out inside large hangars and more care was given to the salting processes, thus improving the traditional staple of the fisheries. Other products were also introduced or reintroduced, especially tinned fish, fish meal and fish oil. Tinned fish required fairly sophisticated equipment and was sold mainly in Italy and North Africa.[11] Exports of fish from Moçâmedes thus picked up rapidly in the 1920s, to reach a value of £133,000 in 1926.[12] However,

---

[2] Vilela, 1923; Nascimento, 1898, pp. 12–15, 55–56; Guimarães and Paiva, 1942.
[3] Vilela, 1923, pp. 32, 401; Monteiro, 1968, II, p. 207.
[4] Nascimento, 1892, pp. 28–29.   [5] Vilela, 1923, pp. 404–405.
[6] See graphs.   [7] *C de M*, 31, March 1905, and 32, May 1905.
[8] FO, *AS*, 3928, 1907.
[9] AHU, 1R–16P, Capello to Minister 21/9/1896.   [10] *C de M*, 32, May 1905.
[11] Vilela, 1923; Guimarães and Paiva, 1942; Carneiro, 1934.   [12] See graphs.

during the Great Depression of the early 1930s, thousands of kilos of fish were once more thrown into the sea as markets collapsed everywhere.[13]

In a rather different category was the ephemeral development of whaling. From about 1909, Norwegian and British whalers began to establish shore factories in south-western Africa for the processing of their catches. This led to a phenomenal boom in the exports of Moçâmedes between 1911 and 1915, which brought in quite untypical profits to the state and nearly succeeded in eliminating southern Angola's chronic trade deficit. But this boom was very short-lived, for the war and the development of factory-ships combined to reduce the activities of shore factories to a very modest level after 1915.[14]

Apart from the fishing industry, there was also a small textile industry, which flourished on the coast from the 1850s to the 1890s. Work on the first plant was started by a German settler in 1857, and he was joined by a Portuguese entrepreneur in the early 1860s.[15] By 1886, the two factories were producing goods of high quality, valued at £2,000, although the machinery employed was archaic.[16] The cloth was aimed entirely at the African market, and most of it was transported with dried fish to the Congo estuary to be sold.[17] However, these two factories were not using local raw cotton to make thread, but were importing it from England.[18] They were thus ruined by the 1892 tariffs, which made imports from foreign countries prohibitively expensive and were aimed at protecting the Angolan market exclusively for the metropolitan textile industry.[19]

The second major branch of production in the colonial nucleus was agriculture, although it must be stressed again that southern Angola was in general poorly suited to agriculture. The aridity of the climate, the infertility of the soils, and the lack of good communications combined to limit plantations and farms to a few small oases in the coastal strip, some valleys in the highlands, and very occasional points along the middle Cunene river. The south was always of little agricultural importance within the colony as a whole, and the myth of its agricultural potential was based more on climatic advantages for white settlement than on any strictly economic criteria.

Cotton was generally the main plantation crop, and it received official encouragement from the 1850s.[20] The first spectacular development in cotton production came about as a result of the civil war in the United States. The price of cotton in southern Angola shot up to reach a peak of

[13] Azevedo, 1945, p. 144.
[14] Azevedo, 1945, passim; AHA, Av–41–83–7, GM, Relatório, 30/9/1912.
[15] Azevedo, 1945, p. 152; Felner, 1940, III, p. 130.
[16] FO, *AS*, 584, 1889.   [17] FO, *AS*, 584, 1889; Sousa, 1887, p. 399.
[18] Botelho, 1890.   [19] Azevedo, 1945, p. 153.
[20] Alves, 1970, pp. 132–137.

about 15p per kilo in 1863, and every available inch of land was planted with cotton. Exports in 1861 had only been worth £200, but by 1865 they had reached £13,800. Prices fell steadily after the end of the civil war in 1864, but they remained high enough to encourage production, and the maximum export level of £14,900 was reached in 1874.[21] But prices continued to fall, and production slumped after 1874. From the mid-1870s to the late 1900s, prices fluctuated between about 2p and 4p per kilo, and the normal value of cotton exports from Moçâmedes fell to less than £1,000 around the turn of the century.[22] Problems of depressed prices were made worse by the degeneration of cotton plants, the exhaustion of the soil and a bad series of drought years in the 1900s.[23]

Cotton production picked up in a slow and erratic fashion from the late 1900s, owing to a number of factors. Prices rose steadily on the world market until 1920 and remained generally high in the 1920s in spite of violent fluctuations.[24] Portuguese industrialists were becoming increasingly interested in colonial cotton supplies and the government introduced a number of financial inducements for cotton planters.[25] In southern Angola, the area under cotton cultivation also increased slightly, for better communications and greater military security permitted the setting up of a few plantations in the Cunene valley.[26] The high point in exports was reached in 1920, when prices were at their maximum, but the export value of £7,200 was still only about half of the previous peak in 1874.[27]

The failure of cotton exports to recover former levels was due largely to a diversification of agricultural production. Sugar cane had been grown since the 1850s for transformation into *aguardente* (firewater or rum), which was mainly used for trade in the interior.[28] A measure of protection was granted to the Moçâmedes *aguardente* producers from the beginning, but the competition from cheap 'Hamburg gin' was very severe.[29] Protection was enormously increased in 1892 and 1895, so that foreign alcohol was virtually excluded from the colony.[30] Sugar cane plantations expanded rapidly in the 1890s in southern Angola, replacing cotton in many areas and even spreading on a small scale to the Huíla highlands.[31]

But the boom in *aguardente* production was short-lived. International pressure was brought to bear on Portugal during the 1900s to enforce the decisions of various international conferences which had addressed themselves to the suppression of alcoholism in Africa.[32] At the same time,

[21] Torres, 1952. [22] *Estatística Commercial*, 1909, pp. xvi–xvii.
[23] Nascimento, 1898, p. 59; Almeida, 1912, p. 544.
[24] Munro, 1976, p. 148. [25] FO, *AS*, 5143, 1913, and 5402, 1914.
[26] Braz, 1918, pp. 134–135. [27] See graphs; Munro, 1976, p. 148.
[28] Alves, 1970, pp. 112–137. [29] Alves, 1970, pp. 141–142.
[30] Coutinho, 1910, p. 8.
[31] *Commercio de Mossamedes*, 28/2/1909; Pimentel, 1903, p. 84.
[32] Coutinho, 1910.

metropolitan pressure groups demanded that the colonial market be reserved for Portuguese wine, which being of a lower alcoholic content was not subjected to the same restrictions.[33] The combination of these rather contradictory pressures led to the final suppression of *aguardente* production in 1911.[34] The Moçâmedes planters attempted to convert to sugar production, but they quickly succumbed to the fierce competition from Benguela and Luanda for the limited sugar quota imported by Portugal on preferential terms.[35]

Other crops were tried by the planters, but never with very great success. In the early years, labourers from the plantations and fisheries were employed to collect orchilia, a lichen from which blue dyes were manufactured and which grew in arid regions affected by sea air.[36] Orchilia exports reached a peak value of £1,500 in 1858 and rose again in the 1880s to reach an export value of £3,500 in 1884 and 1885.[37] But cheap chemical substitutes undermined the market for this product, and exports fell away from the 1890s.[38] Another product of the coastal oases was *almeidina* (potato-gum), in effect a very inferior kind of rubber, drawn from a cactus type of plant used for hedges. It first reached a satisfactory price in 1887, and small amounts were exported during the rubber boom of the 1890s and 1900s. However, the annual value of *almeidina* exports never rose above £3,000.[39] Finally, one should mention that small amounts of coffee, cocoa and sisal were grown at various times, although these never progressed beyond the experimental stage.[40]

Much more important than ephemeral booms in tropical cash crops was the steady growth of the production of foodstuffs. The victualling of passing ships provided an early market, especially important in the 1840s and 1850s, when American whalers and British anti-slavery cruisers were numerous in southern waters.[41] But the fundamental market for foodstuffs was provided by the steadily growing needs of the fisheries. Many plantations specialized in the production of sweet potatoes. which were dried and used as the basis of the diet of labourers in the fisheries.[42] Another market was provided by the growing settler population of officials, entrepreneurs, army officers, missionaries and so forth, a market which was

[33] Teixeira, 1934, pp. 353–355. [34] FO, *AS*, 4903, 1912.
[35] Couceiro, 1910, pp. 293–297, 408.
[36] Monteiro, 1968, II, pp. 184–185.
[37] Torres, 1950, p. 445; AHU, 2R–8P, Mapa 26/1/1885 and 2R–10P, Mapa 26/1/1886.
[38] FO, *AS*, 1105, 1892.
[39] Portugal, 1897, pp. 50–51, 71; Geraldes and Fragateiro, 1910, pp. 73–75; *BO*, 1913, Apenso 27.
[40] See entries for various years of *Estatística Commercial*.
[41] Felner, 1940, III, pp. 89–90; Livingstone, 1963, I, p. 153.
[42] Nascimento, 1898, p. 58.

25

mainly catered for by the wheat, fruit and vegetables grown in the highlands.[43]

Lastly, it should be noted that extensive stock raising was also of some importance in the colonial nucleus. Sheep failed to prosper in the region, in spite of various attempts to develop commercial wool farming.[44] But cattle were well adapted, and in the early 1890s it was estimated that the settlers owned about 8,000 head.[45] However, the great majority of cattle and cattle products exported from Moçâmedes came from the African peasant societies, and this topic will thus be covered in a later chapter. The stock owned by settlers was mainly reserved for more specialized purposes: dairy production, ploughing, working of irrigation pumps, and, most important of all, transport riding.[46] Large-scale cattle ranching for export only developed in the 1920s, after the final conquest and 'pacification' of the Ovambo flood plain.[47]

Apart from fishing and agriculture, various 'service industries' assumed particular prominence in the economy of the colonial nucleus of southern Angola. The major activities involved comprised transport riding, mercenary service, commerce and bureaucratic employment. Little need be said about the latter, except that there was a tendency for the government artificially to increase the size of the local bureaucracy in order to provide employment for state-subsidized immigrants who failed to make a living in agriculture.[48]

Transport riding developed after the arrival of Boer immigrants from the Transvaal in the 1880s. The Boers rapidly took over the transportation business from head-porters, who had always been particularly hard to come by in the sparsely populated southern steppes. Business remained on a modest scale in the 1880s, being limited chiefly to ivory from Ovamboland and cotton from the plantations at the foot of the escarpment.[49] The Boers also made money as road-builders, opening up and improving tracks from Benguela and Moçâmedes into the interior.[50]

The real boom in transport riding occurred in the 1890s and 1900s, when large quantities of root rubber began to be exported from eastern Angola. The chronic shortage of head-porters became acute, and the wagoners moved in to fill the gap. Transport by ox-wagon was slower and up to 50% more expensive than by free head-porter, but the need for transport was so great that wagons provided the only solution.[51] The prevalence of tsetse fly over much of northern and central Angola limited

[43] Almeida, 1912, pp. 299, 555–561.   [44] Postma, 1897, p. 236.
[45] Nascimento, 1892, statistical tables.
[46] Postma, 1897, pp. 235–243; Botelho, 1890.
[47] Teixeira, 1934, pp. 666–667.   [48] *J de M*, 1/12/1892.
[49] AHA, Av–41–82–7, GM, Relatório 8/10/1883.
[50] Postma, 1897, pp. 244–246.   [51] Angola, 1910, pp. 59–61.

the activities of the ox-wagons, but they nevertheless ranged all over eastern and southern Angola, and deep into British or Belgian territory beyond.[52]

However, transport riding was ruined in the 1910s and 1920s. The rubber boom came to an end in the early 1910s, and the demand for transport in the interior fell correspondingly. At the same time, the early successes of the Boers led to an overproduction of wagons and cut-throat competition for the declining market.[53] This was compounded by the slow penetration inland of the Benguela and Moçâmedes railways, from 1902 and 1905 respectively.[54] But the worst blow of all came with the introduction of lorries and motor roads from 1915 onwards.[55] By 1917, the price of transporting 15 kilos of goods from the Huíla highlands to Moçâmedes by wagon had fallen to 13p, when it had remained steady at between 22½p and 25p since the 1880s.[56] By the late 1920s, wagoning had been reduced to a very local and relatively unimportant activity.[57]

Lorries could not bring the same prosperity as wagons to the colonial nucleus of southern Angola, for lorries did not require the very special conditions which had made the southern highlands a major transport base for much of the colony. The southern highlands combined the advantages for transport riding of good cattle country for rearing transport oxen and plentiful supplies of wood for the building and repairing of wagons.[58] With the advent of lorries, such natural advantages disappeared. Some people continued to make a living from driving and hiring out lorries, but the south no longer serviced the wide area which it had once done in the heyday of transport riding.[59]

Mercenary service on colonial expeditions was even more lucrative than transport riding, but it was much more irregular as a source of income. Military 'auxiliaries' were paid a daily wage, usually £1 from the 1890s, plus extra bonuses for horses and wagons. Compensation was guaranteed for any loss of property, and ammunition was supplied by the government. The auxiliaries only had to bring or hunt for their own food. In addition, half of all looted cattle were handed over to the mercenaries. As in the case of transport riding, the semi-professional mercenaries of Angola were mainly based in the southern highlands but were used widely on campaigns in southern, central and eastern Angola. But this

---

[52] Heese, 1976, map between pp. 91 and 92; NAZ, BS2–102, Administrator to High Commissioner 6/3/1903.
[53] Almeida, 1912, pp. 289, 302.
[54] Portugal, 1912; AHA, Av–41–83–7, GM, Relatório 30/9/1912.
[55] Van der Merwe, 1951, p. 21.
[56] Portugal, 1918, I, p. 392; prices for earlier years are scattered abundantly through the sources.
[57] Galvão, 1930, p. 100.   [58] Postma, 1897, p. 243.
[59] Galvão, 1930, pp. 97–100.

lucrative profession, closely tied to transport riding, also declined from the 1910s, when the last of the great colonial campaigns in Angola took place.[60]

Hunting, wood cutting and prospection were subsidiary activities closely linked to mercenary service and transport riding, although not really 'service industries'. They also became part of the economy of the colonial nucleus after the arrival of the Boer trekkers in 1881. Ivory, ostrich feathers, skins and dried meat were the major products of hunting. There was a modest boom in the export of the first two commodities in the 1880s, reaching a peak of £4,500 in 1882, although it is not clear how much of this was due to the activities of Boer hunters.[61] Wood cutting was important not only for the building and maintenance of wagons, but also for a small furniture industry in the highlands.[62] Prospecting was occasionally successful, especially panning for alluvial gold in the Cassinga area.[63] But none of these activities were generally remunerative enough to be carried on in their own right, and they tended to be practised in the course of transport riding.[64]

Commerce was a particularly widespread and pervasive activity throughout the colonial nucleus, from the wandering Boer hunter who bartered dried meat for maize to the big import–export houses of Moçâmedes. The trading structure will be considered in later chapters on colonial society and peasant production, but it needs to be noted here that most of the entrepreneurs in the colonial nucleus were as involved in trade as in production. Indeed, it was often the profits of trade with African societies which were reinvested in plantations and fisheries.[65]

Having briefly surveyed the branches of production in the colonial nucleus, it remains to consider the overarching structures of labour and capital, beginning with the latter. Unfortunately, it has not proved possible to obtain statistical data on the amounts of capital invested, and it is not even possible to make any kind of estimates. However, it seems clear that capital resources were concentrated in a few hands from the very outset. A handful of rich settlers, the Banco Nacional Ultramarino after 1864 and a few outside companies after 1894 controlled all the available credit and owned most of the means of production.[66] The great majority of the southern settlers were 'poor whites', who arrived with little or no capital and almost invariably fell into debt.

Debt was a particular problem in the fisheries. Most of the immigrant

[60] Postma, 1897, pp. 243–244; Van der Merwe, 1951, pp. 75–77; Heese, 1976, p. 269; Dias, 1943.   [61] Postma, 1897, pp. 246–248; *BO*, 43, 26/10/1885.
[62] Van der Merwe, 1951, p. 4.   [63] AHA, Av–31–7–5, GH to GG 17/5/1902.
[64] Statham, 1922, p. 146.   [65] See chapter 4, pp. 49–51.
[66] Couceiro, 1910, pp. 359–377.

fishermen were desperately poor and received no state aid, while the costs which they incurred in the desert environment were extremely high. Everything, even water in most ports, had to be imported from elsewhere, and the cost of a modest wooden house and a small fishing boat came to about £320 in 1894.[67] The fishermen were forced to sell their fish at artificially low prices and buy their supplies at artificially inflated prices from their merchant creditors in Moçâmedes, and they were thus rarely able to pay off their initial debt. Indeed, their situation was essentially one of debt peonage.[68]

The tendency in the fishing industry was for increasing concentration of ownership[69] and fiercely contested attempts by foreign and metropolitan capital to take over the industry. In 1891, an outside company was rumoured to be thinking of introducing steamers and reorganizing the industry, and the government had to ban steamers in order to pacify the outraged fishermen.[70] A similar move by a British company with West African connections in 1904 was also foiled.[71] The Companhia de Moçâmedes was permitted to invest a little in fishing, but only on condition that traditional methods were used.[72] Even as late as the 1920s and 1930s, the prohibition on motorized trawlers was severely hampering outside investment.[73] Nevertheless, metropolitan capital became involved in the southern Angolan fisheries from about 1910, originally because of the whaling boom, and in about 1920 the Belgian Société Générale set up a fishing company under the name of Angopeixe, with a nominal capital of £100,000.[74]

Debt and capital concentration were also marked in the agricultural sector, for plantations required considerable capital investment in land, slaves, irrigation pumps and other machinery. Plantations were usually mortgaged to the hilt, and every drought or slump in commodity prices led to a spate of bankruptcies and further concentration of landed property. However, the Banco Nacional Ultramarino was embarrassed by all the land which fell into its hands in this way, and sold most or all of it to wealthy settlers, so that very litle land fell permanently under the control of metropolitan capital.[75] As for foreign capital, the Companhia de Moçâmedes set up cotton plantations in the middle Cunene valley in the 1900s, which were responsible for about 70% of Moçâmedes' very

[67] Nascimento, 1898, pp. 12–15, 55–56.   [68] Castilho, 1899, pp. 234–235.
[69] AHU, 1R–23P, GG to Minister 25/1/1914.
[70] AHU, 2R–16P, GG to Minister 15/12/1891.
[71] FO, *AS*, 3478, 1905.   [72] *P em A*, 15, March 1895, p. 541.
[73] Vilela, 1923, pp. 365–369; Guimarães and Paiva, 1942, pp. 14, 16.
[74] Vilela, 1923, pp. 270–275, 284, 304–305, 317–318, 326, 411; Machado, 1918, p. 296; Bullock, 1932, p. 27.
[75] Giraúl, 1910, p. 14; Viúva Bastos, 1913, pp. 16–17.

limited exports of cotton in that year. However, these cotton plantations had gone out of production by 1929.[76] The Companhia de Moçâmedes was also in the forefront of the development of cattle ranching during the 1920s.[77] But these activities were situated on the periphery of the colonial nucleus, and foreign capital was rare in the core area.

Capital concentration and debt were less pronounced in the service industries, which had the advantage of not being affected by large initial outlays on labour or land. But the cost of a wagon and a span of thirty oxen in the mid-1890s stood at around £250,[78] while a rifle and a salted horse might cost over £100.[79] Many traders also had to buy their initial stock of trading goods on credit and remained permanently in debt.[80]

Before examining the labour situation in the colonial nucleus, it is imperative to begin with some definitions, for the literature on labour relations in the Portuguese colonies has tended to be obscured by a very imprecise use of language. Slavery is defined for the purposes of this chapter in a strictly economic sense to denote the system whereby workers are bought and sold as commodities. Proletarian wage-labour is characterized by the separation of the workers from the means of production and the resulting necessity for them to sell their labour-power. Forced labour exists where the state intervenes to compel the workers to labour for the state or to sell their labour-power to entrepreneurs. Serf labour is that rendered in return for the right to use the means of production owned by the employer.

Slavery was the dominant form of labour relations in the colonial nucleus of southern Angola from 1840 to 1878. The effective suppression of the Atlantic slave trade in the 1840s led to a glut of locally available slaves and a steep fall in the price of slaves.[81] At the same time, the indigenous population of the coastal strip in the south was very small and very mobile and quite unable to satisfy the labour needs of the plantations and fisheries.[82] The settlers thus imported slaves by sea from the traditional exporting ports along the Angolan coast.[83]

Slavery continued to be predominant in the economy of the southern colonial nucleus between 1879 and 1911, even though the institution was legally abolished throughout the Portuguese colonies by a law of 1875, which was to take effect after three years. In law, contract labourers (*serviçaes*, singular *serviçal*) were to take the place of slaves. However, it is essential to distinguish between legal forms and economic realities. In effect, a combination of legal loopholes and administrative connivances

[76] AHA, Av–41–83–7, GM Relatório 30/9/1912; Galvão, 1930, p. 177.
[77] Teixeira, 1934, p. 667.   [78] Nascimento, 1898, pp. 78–79.
[79] Möller, 1974, pp. 32. 112.   [80] Almeida, 1912, pp. 529–534.
[81] Livingstone, 1959, II, p. 253.   [82] Amaral, 1880, p. 7.
[83] Amaral, 1880, p. 30; Nascimento, 1898, p. 60.

permitted slavery to continue.[84] The crux of the problem lay in the un-willingness or inability of the Portuguese government to pay compensation to the slaveholders, unlike the British government in South Africa in the 1830s.[85] Lisbon thus played a double game, pacifying international philanthropic pressure groups by a façade of abolition, while saving the planters and fishermen from ruin by allowing *de facto* slavery to continue.

There were three fundamental mechanisms which were used to guarantee the survival of slavery in spite of the law of 1875. In the first place, all freed slaves had to sign an initial contract for a maximum of five years with their redeemers. This provision of the law was used not only to bind ex-slaves to their former masters, but also to enable the continued buying of slaves from African dealers, the price of purchase being now described in humanitarian terms as the cost of redeeming slaves from barbaric servitude.[86] The second mechanism, which was formally illegal, consisted in automatic re-contracting at the end of the five-year period. In spite of a number of hesitations and protests in Angola and in Lisbon, the colonial authorities insisted that a blind eye be turned to this practice in order to save the slaveholders from ruin.[87] Thirdly, a market for slaves was maintained by the practice of sub-contracting for a fee. This was also formally illegal, but the state was itself one of the worst offenders, sub-contracting large numbers of *serviçaes* from the settlers in order to build the Moçâmedes railway.[88]

The main problem facing the slaveholders in Moçâmedes in the period 1879 to 1911 was that the price of *serviçaes* was increasing very rapidly, as can be seen from the accompanying table:

Prices of slaves and serviçaes on the coast in sterling

1830s ?	11–13[89]
1854	1.5–3[90]
1874	3–5[91]
1882	4–6[92]
1894	8–12[93]
1905	11–30[94]

This inflation in the price of redeeming slaves on the coast was due to the

[84] Duffy, 1967.   [85] *J de M*, 24/10/1881.   [86] Giraúl, 1912, pp. 11–12.
[87] AHU, 1R–4P, GG Relatório 9/4/1884; AHU, 2R–7P, CG to Minister 16/8/1884; AHU, 2R–13P, GG to Minister 16/1/1889 and marginal notes DGU and Minister.
[88] AHA, Av–41–83–7, GM Relatório 30/9/1912.
[89] Livingstone, 1959, II, p. 253.   [90] Livingstone, 1959, II, p. 253.
[91] Monteiro, 1968, II, p. 40.   [92] Hammond, 1966, p. 317.
[93] Nascimento, 1898, p. 60.   [94] *C de M*, 27, January 1905.

tremendous demand for labour from the cocoa plantations of São Tomé from the 1880s.[95] Local entrepreneurs in Moçâmedes could no longer compete with the planters of São Tomé, and during the fishing and *aguardente* slump of the 1900s imports of slave labour into Moçâmedes came to a virtual halt.[96] However, one aspect of these rising prices was that some enterprising Moçâmedes settlers began to export *serviçaes* to São Tomé.[97] State demand for labour for the Moçâmedes railway from 1905 also provided a lucrative market.[98]

Although slavery dominated the economy of the colonial nucleus up to 1911, there were also two subordinate types of labour relations which co-existed with slavery. On the one hand, there was a certain amount of proletarian wage-labour. This was of varied origin, including freed slaves, immigrant Cabinda sailors from northern Angola, and impoverished whites and *mestiços*. In general terms, these wage-earners formed a skilled labour aristocracy, in an intermediary position between the masters and the slaves.[99] On the other hand, there was some serf labour exacted from the indigenous inhabitants who had been dispossessed of their lands by the settlers. These labour services would normally be performed in return for grazing rights and would usually be rendered at peak moments in the agricultural or fishing years.[100] Lastly, it should be noted that although forced labour was legally established throughout the Portuguese empire in 1899, it was not applied in southern Angola before 1911.[101]

When the republican authorities finally abolished slavery in southern Angola between 1911 and 1913, the transition to proletarian wage-labour was smoother than had been expected.[102] Slavery had in fact prepared the ground for wage-labour. This was partly because the masters had been forced by the state to pay a token wage to their *serviçaes* after 1880, so that the wage form was in some sense already established.[103] Much more important was the fact that slavery had produced a community which had lost contact with its original homes but which was effectively divorced from the means of production in its new home. In addition, slavery had instilled certain skills and work rhythms which were easily carried over into wage-labour.[104]

But although the ex-slaves provided the core of a stable proletariat after 1911, the rapid expansion in the labour needs of the fisheries in the 1920s led to the use of large amounts of forced labour. The 1911 labour code

[95] *C de M*, 27, January 1905.
[96] AHA, Av–41–83–6, GM Relatório 31/5/1910.
[97] AHA, Av–41–92–1, CG to GG 18/3/1905.
[98] AHA, Av–41–83–7, GM Relatório 30/9/1912.
[99] See chapter 4, pp. 42, 45–47.   [100] Nascimento, 1898, pp. 11, 25.
[101] *Commercio de Mossamedes*, 14/2/1909.   [102] Diniz, 1914, pp. 81–83.
[103] Giraúl, 1912, p. 18.   [104] Vilela, 1923, pp. 395–397.

established two types of forced labour, and this remained fundamentally unchanged up to 1962. The first and the most common type can be called obligatory labour, which was closely linked to taxation. Every male native not only had to pay an annual tax but also had to perform a certain yearly period of salaried work, unless he could prove that he earned a sufficient monetary income in some other way. A distinction was usually made between those who fulfilled their labour obligations without direct state intervention (*voluntários*) and those who actually had to be compelled to 'offer' their services (*contratados*). Apart from this obligatory labour, there also existed forced labour proper, that is unpaid labour for the state on public works.[105]

In southern Angola after 1911, a distinct pattern of forced labour emerged in the colonial nucleus. Agricultural workers were by and large *voluntários*, whereas labourers in the fisheries were mainly *contratados*.[106] Forced labour proper was used extensively for building and repairing motor roads, and also for porterage service on military campaigns.[107] The effects of these new labour demands on African tributary societies will be examined in a later chapter, but it should be noted here that forced labour presented particular problems for the fisheries. The *contratados* were unwilling migrants, many of whom had never seen the sea and were totally unused to any kind of maritime activity. By the time they had acquired some of the elementary skills involved in fishing, their short-term contracts had expired and they returned home. The fishing entrepreneurs were preoccupied with the necessity to stabilize this transient work force around the nucleus of ex-slave proletarians, but salaries and conditions were too poor to persuade workers from the interior to settle permanently in the inhospitable coastal desert. The fisheries were thus the most adversely affected sector by the abolition of quasi-slavery, and this goes a long way towards explaining the particularly strong resistance of southern Angola to the labour reforms of the republic.[108]

Lastly, an attempt can be made to quantify the amounts of labour employed in the economy of the colonial nucleus, although the figures are often partial, contradictory and unreliable. In 1854, the slave population of the south was already about 600 strong. Ten years later, when the cotton boom was in full swing, the number of slaves had risen to nearly 2,500.[109] In the late 1870s, at the end of the cotton boom and during the legal abolition of slavery, there were between 3,000 and 4,000 slaves.[110] By the time the republican authorities finally stamped out slavery in the

[105] Duffy, 1962, pp. 129–134, 182–189. [106] Diniz, 1915, pp. 71–73.
[107] *BG*, XXVIII, 342, 1917, p. 479.
[108] Machado, 1918, p. 299; Guimarães and Paiva, 1942, p. 16.
[109] Silva, 1971–1973, 34, p. 497.
[110] AHU, IR–Diversos, 1868–1888, GM Relatório 19/6/1877.

south in 1913, the total *serviçal* population was put at around 10,000.[111] The introduction of the new system of forced labour led to a sharp increase in the figures to around 30,000 in 1914. However, it must be stressed that this increase was more apparent than real. In the first place it included many workers on contracts of six months or less. Secondly, it included the wage and serf labour which had been excluded from the earlier statistics on the numbers of slaves or *serviçaes*.[112] In the late 1920s, the total labour force was still around 30,000.[113]

The economic history of the colonial nucleus in southern Angola between 1840 and 1926 can thus be summarized as consisting of two related processes. On the one hand, the concentration and intensity of capital investment increased steadily, and fishing emerged as the uncontested motor of the southern economy. On the other hand, the labour employed also increased steadily, and slave relations of production slowly gave way to a more complex system of wage-labour and forced labour. The social and political developments which corresponded to this evolution of the economic base will thus form the subject of the following chapter.

[111] Diniz, 1914, p. 61.   [112] Diniz, 1915, pp. 71–73.
[113] Partial statistics in Galvão, 1930, pp. 154–155; Rates, 1929, p. 61; Cya, 1936, p. 111.

4

Society and politics in the colonial nucleus

The society of the colonial nucleus consisted of three basic classes. At the bottom there were the slaves and their proletarian descendants, characterized by pauperization and total lack of control over the means of production. Above them was a fairly numerous petty bourgeoisie, owning the means of production or receiving a salary over the level of pauperization, but employing little or no labour outside the family unit. At the apex of the social pyramid were the few local capitalists, who enjoyed extensive control over the means of production and were large-scale employers of labour.

This class structure was both reinforced and distorted at the level of class consciousness by a variety of non-economic factors, of which the most important were race, language and religion. These factors helped to strengthen the class alliance between the capitalists and the petty bourgeoisie, so that class struggle was usually expressed ideologically in the simplified form of settlers versus slaves. Factional struggles within the settler group were also expressed in terms of Portuguese against Afrikaners or whites against non-whites. Racial factors were prominent as well in the struggles of the slaves against their masters.

The sources present the slaves and proletarians of colonial society in a very restricted and specific manner. Workers were always objects of discourse, and they usually appeared in the guise of economic or political problems for officials and settlers. Slaves and proletarians appear to have been totally illiterate, and in any case they were systematically kept away from the types of expression which have been preserved in archives and libraries. Missionaries were excluded from most of the colonial nucleus, which was reserved for a secular clergy more concerned with settlers than with slaves.[1] Nor is there any substantial ethnographic monograph or collection of oral data to help to fill the gap.[2] As a result, almost nothing

[1] Brásio, 1966–1971, passim.
[2] For existing material, see Estermann, 1939; Cardoso, 1966.

35

can be said about the perceptions and motivations of the slaves, and the analysis which follows is of necessity somewhat incomplete and unsatisfactory.

Daily life on plantations varied little during the period of slavery. Working hours ran from sunrise to sunset, with a two-hour break in the middle of the day and a day of rest on Sundays. Men and women performed the same tasks and worked in large gangs under the supervision of drivers and overseers, who were usually slaves themselves. Women were more numerous than men, partly because they were said to be more accustomed to agricultural tasks and partly because they were paid less than men after the introduction of token salaries in the late 1870s. Supervisory and skilled slaves could earn up to six times the legal minimum salary, but there is no indication as to what proportion of slaves fell into this category.[3] Housing was provided in large courtyards behind the planters' houses, the high walls being covered with broken glass to prevent escapes.[4] The diet was monotonous, based on dried sweet potatoes and a little dried fish.[5] Most planters also ran a small store, at which the *serviçaes* spent most of their tiny salaries on alcohol.[6]

Conditions in the fisheries were worse than on plantations, and labour relations tended to be more difficult. The quality of food and drinking water was very poor in the isolated ports, where both these commodities had to be brought by sea from the oases. Housing was also wretched because of the lack of building materials in the desert and the expenses incurred in importing them. Scurvy and other diseases were therefore rife.[7] Sex ratios were very uneven, with a high preponderance of men over women. This was because men were used for fishing operations, whereas women were only employed in the less labour-consuming activities of drying and salting.[8] Furthermore, most of the slaves were brought from the interior of northern and central Angola and were totally unaccustomed to the desert and the sea.[9]

Conditions varied somewhat according to specific ports, but the worst conditions were undoubtedly to be encountered in the isolated settlement of the Baía dos Tigres in the far south. The fishing was richest of all here, but particular local problems required large boats and complex nets. All the fisheries were thus well equipped and were mostly owned by

---

[3] Postma, 1897, pp. 233–235; Nascimento, 1898, pp. 57–58; Giraúl, 1912, pp. 12–21; Staatsargief, Pretoria, A779–I, Botha Papers, Contractos.

[4] Möller, 1974, p. 24.

[5] AHA, Av–41–92–1, CG to GG 18/3/1905; Nascimento, 1892, pp. 28–29.

[6] Möller, 1974, p. 24; AHU, 2R–4P, CG to Minister, 12/10/1880.

[7] Nascimento, 1898, pp. 12–15, 55; FO, *AS*, 584, 1889; AHU, 1R–16P, Capello to Minister 21/9/1896.

[8] Vilela, 1923, pp. 221, 339.   [9] Amaral, 1880, p. 30.

wealthy absentee proprietors.[10] The little village lay on a low sand spit opposite a desolate shore of shifting sand dunes, with no vegetation to be seen for miles around. Drinking water was brought in sailing boats for the few resident whites, but the *serviçaes* were made to drink from a foul well on the mainland. They had no fresh fruit or vegetables in their diet and they were housed in revolting 'baracoons'.[11] A water distiller was set up in 1899, but it was constantly breaking down and was finally left to rust from 1905 to 1923.[12]

Apart from the slaves in agriculture and fishing, there were a certain number employed in domestic service, commerce, workshops and public works. In 1914, as many as 30% of the workers were employed in these sectors, although the figures were probably artificially boosted by the numbers working on the railway.[13] The settlers complained that *serviçaes* employed by the state were treated scandalously well, but there are no other indications as to conditions in these sectors.[14] Lastly, it should be noted that the geographical distribution of slaves was uneven. The great majority were located on the coast, whereas there were few in the highlands.[15]

The slaves were far from being passive victims, and the labour history of the south was one of constant struggle. The most common reaction of the slaves was to escape, by sea or land. Some slaves returned to their societies of origin or integrated themselves into another society.[16] But many others joined bandit groups in the rugged lands of the escarpment and returned to wreak vengeance on their former masters.[17] However, social banditry was a complex phenomenon in southern Angola. The majority of the bandits were local Africans who had lost their lands to the white settlers, and this will therefore be dealt with in a subsequent chapter.

Although flight was the most common form of slave response, resistance from within colonial society was also widespread. Internal resistance was usually closely related to administrative changes in the labour system. Every time that there was some kind of modification of labour legislation, the slaves would do all in their power to maximize the practical effects of such modifications. Indeed, it is interesting to note how quickly the slaves got to know of proposed or actual changes in labour laws.[18] However, the southern slaves never seem to have themselves initiated any major changes

[10] Nascimento, 1898, pp. 14–15.
[11] AHU, 1R–16P, Capello to Minister 21/9/1896.
[12] AHA, Av–41–72–5, GM to GG 15/9/1899; AHMH, 15, Codex GM 1900–1901, GM to Inspector da Fazenda Provincial 10/11/1900; Azevedo, 1958, p. 402.
[13] Diniz, 1915, p. 73. [14] Giraúl, 1912, p. 24.
[15] Diniz, 1915, p. 73. [16] AHU, 1R–4P, GG, Relatório 9/4/1884.
[17] Clarence-Smith, 1976 a, p. 220.
[18] AHU, 46P, CG to Minister, 29/7/1876.

in legislation by their acts of resistance. Changes were the result of international pressure,[19] or of events in other parts of Angola, such as the Bailundo Revolt of 1902.[20]

In 1869, a decree was passed whereby all remaining slaves in Angola had to be given the very ambiguous status of *libertos*. The distinction between a slave and a *liberto* was a hard one to make. Effectively, a *liberto* was no more than a slave who was guaranteed that he would be free by 1879.[21] But it seems that this measure was interpreted by some slaves in Moçâmedes as meaning immediate and total liberation. The 1869 decree was thus followed by a wave of 'insubordination' among the servile population of the south.[22]

A much more serious crisis occurred during the ten years which followed the decree of 1875, which laid down that slavery was to be totally abolished throughout the Portuguese empire within three years.[23] In 1876, the chief labour inspector attempted to begin the process in Moçâmedes whereby slaves had to sign an initial obligatory five-year contract with their former masters. But he met with great resistance, for the slaves insisted that they be given their *cartas de liberdade* (certificates of manumission) and refused to sign the contracts. Of the 251 contracts passed in Moçâmedes province up to July 1876, only four were established voluntarily.[24] Furthermore, the law of 1875 and subsequent regulations had laid down that the contract workers should receive a minimum monthly wage of about 27p, plus food and lodging. However, strong settler protest had led to this figure being reduced for Moçâmedes and other localities to about 13p for men and 9p for women. This was also extremely unpopular with the slaves, who knew that the original figure had been maintained for Benguela province.[25] During 1877 and 1878, incidents between slaves and masters multiplied and the authorities appear to have abandoned the attempt to have contracts signed.[26]

The crisis came to a head in 1879, when the three-year transition period had expired and the authorities finally had to impose contracts on all remaining slaves. Discontent seethed throughout the region, occasionally flaring up into open violence.[27] The new governor of Moçâmedes appointed to deal with this explosive situation was a dynamic and ambitious young naval officer, Francisco Ferreira do Amaral, later to

[19] Duffy, 1967.
[20] *C de M*, 25, January 1905.
[21] Duffy, 1962, pp. 69, 130.
[22] Silva, 1971–1973, pp. 513–514.
[23] Duffy, 1967, pp. 5–7 and passim.
[24] AHU, 46P, CG to Minister 29/7/1876.
[25] Felner, 1940, I, pp. 74–75, 81–82.
[26] AHU, 2R–3P, CG to Minister 1/2/1877; AHU, 1R, Diversos 1868–1888, GM Relatório 16/7/1879.
[27] AHU, 1R, Diversos 1868–1888, GM Relatório 16/7/1879.

become governor general of Angola, minister for overseas affairs and prime minister.[28] Amaral was unsympathetic to the slaves' cause and decided on a show of strength. On the basis of a denunciation and of his own very imperfect knowledge of the Kimbundu language, Amaral chose to believe that a great conspiracy was on foot in one of the larger plantations, with the aim of starting a slave rebellion and killing all whites.[29] A detachment of soldiers was therefore sent to the plantation at dawn, to seize the six 'ring-leaders' and give them from 600 to 1,000 lashes each. All six were then to be deported to São Tomé, although it would appear that two of them subsequently died from their wounds.[30]

Although this show of force appears to have discouraged any acts of open rebellion, Amaral's actions had been quite illegal and he was replaced in 1880 by the more liberal José Bento Ferreira de Almeida, later to have a brilliant parliamentary career and to become minister for overseas affairs.[31] Almeida was much more sympathetic to the plight of the slaves and attempted to ensure a real transition from slavery to free contract labour. During his few months in office, he toured the plantations and fisheries enforcing the payment of wages in cash, prosecuting settlers found guilty of torture and encouraging the slaves to lay all their complaints before him.[32] But Almeida came up against the constant hostility of the settlers and was revolted by the connivance of certain officials and the leniency of judges towards settlers convicted of homicide and torture. As a result, he resigned in June 1880.[33]

Almeida was replaced by the settlers' choice, Sebastião Nunes da Matta, who reverted to the much more repressive policies of Amaral. Violence immediately flared up again. In December 1880 there was a riot involving some 200 *serviçaes* and leaving nine people seriously wounded.[34] At some time in 1880 or 1881, five young white girls were also said to have been raped and killed by a band of *serviçaes*.[35] Under Matta's harsh rule, the slaves ceased to bring their complaints to the authorities and resorted instead to flight and bandit raids on their former masters.[36] There was however a kind of lull in 1883, as both slaves and masters waited to see what would happen when the bulk of the initial five-year obligatory

---

[28] *Grande Enciclopédia Portuguesa e Brasileira*, XI, pp. 195–196.
[29] Amaral, 1880, pp. 13–16.
[30] Amaral, 1880, pp. 19–21; AHU, 1R–1P, Publica Forma 3/2/1879.
[31] AHU, 2R–4P, GM to Minister 15/2/1880; *Grande Enciclopédia Portuguesa e Brasileira*, II, p. 55.
[32] AHU, 2R–4P, GM to Minister 15/4/1880.
[33] AHU, 1R, Diversos 1868–1888, GM to DGU 14/6/1880.
[34] AHA, Av–41–70–1, GM to GG 11/1/1881.
[35] *J de M*, 20/8/1881.
[36] AHA, Cod–A–8–4, GG to Minister 5/5/1883.

39

contracts expired in 1884.[37] In the meanwhile, vagrancy regulations were used to deal with those whose contracts expired earlier.[38]

In 1884, both the chief labour inspector and Amaral, now governor general, decided that the law would have to be 'bent' in favour of the settlers. Rather than allowing the *serviçaes* to choose their masters freely, it was decided that the first five-year contracts would be 'automatically prolonged'.[39] When the slaves realized that their long promised freedom was yet again being denied them, and this time in flagrant violation of the law, further violence broke out. Amaral came to southern Angola in person to deal with the situation. He had 400 'ring-leaders' seized and shipped off as soldiers to Mozambique, replacing them with an equal number of docile recently 'freed' and contracted slaves from Novo Redondo.[40]

After this final denial of freedom and brutal repression, the struggles of the *serviçaes* within the colonial nucleus tended to die down. The governor general anticipated trouble in 1889, when the bulk of the contracts were 'automatically prolonged' for the second time, but there is no indication that any violence occurred.[41] A new set of labour regulations were promulgated in 1902, as a result of the Bailundo Revolt, which in the main repeated the regulations of 1880 but tried to see that they were enforced. There were subsequently reports of 'indiscipline' among the Moçâmedes *serviçaes*, especially as a zealous young labour inspector attempted to apply the new regulations and encouraged the slaves to bring their complaints to him.[42] But by 1905, the settlers had managed to obtain the suspension of the regulations for Moçâmedes and the transfer of the labour inspector to the Congo province.[43]

In fact, the outcome of the events of 1875 to 1884 seems to have convinced the *serviçaes* that no more could be gained by violent or legal means from within the system. Nevertheless, the slaves had gained two small concessions. They were paid their tiny token salaries, if at times in kind or in paper bonds redeemable only at their masters' stores, and they were spared the worst excesses of physical coercion.[44] The settlers tried to

[37] AHA, Av–41–82–7, GM Relatório 8/10/1883.
[38] Heese, 1976, p. 17.
[39] AHU, 1R–4P, GG Relatório 9/4/1884; AHU, 2R–7P, CG to Minister 16/8/1884.
[40] Oliveira, 1968–1971, II, pp. 500–594, quoting speech by Almeida in parliament 20/1/1885. Almeida's accusations are denied in AHU, 1R–5P, GG to Minister 26/3/1885, but confirmed in AHU, 2R–7P, CG to Minister 16/8/1884 and in AHM, 5P–23, GG to Chefe Novo Redondo 6/5/1884 and 7/4/1884.
[41] AHU, 2R–13P, GG to Minister 16/1/1889.
[42] AHA, Av–41–92–1, CG to GG 18/3/1905.
[43] AHA, Av–41–92–1, CG to GG 18/3/1905.
[44] Postma, 1897, pp. 233–234.

annul these concessions in a variety of ways, and they could often count on the passivity or sympathy of local officials.[45] But the *serviçaes* were protected by a widespread system of denunciations, whereby a settler who accused his neighbour of a breach of labour regulations could hope to have the *serviçaes* in question transferred to himself.[46] The slaves were also protected by the anxiety of the authorities in Lisbon that a minimum of abuses be available to stoke the fires of the international abolition campaign.[47]

The situation changed dramatically after the republican revolution of 1910. A wave of hope ran through the servile population of Angola, as it appeared that the new authorities were genuinely concerned to stamp out slavery.[48] Agitation was particularly intense in Moçâmedes province, where quasi-slavery appears to have maintained itself more completely and systematically than in other areas of Angola.[49] In one fishery, the *serviçaes* went on strike, and everywhere the slaves clamoured for their liberation.[50] The new governor of Moçâmedes, Carvalhal Correia Henriques, attempted to replace slavery by free contract labour and encouraged the *serviçaes* to lay their complaints before him. But the settlers fought back, and managed to use their influence in Lisbon to have Henriques suspended in January 1912.[51]

But early in 1913, the new governor general, José Norton de Matos, decided to root out the relics of slavery in Moçâmedes once and for all. Commissions were sent to every plantation and fishery to annul existing contracts and to ensure that the *serviçae*s were able freely to choose their masters or set up as independent producers. Repatriation to their original homes was also guaranteed, if the *serviçaes* so desired, but vagrancy was strictly forbidden.[52] The authorities and the settlers were in total disagreement as to the results of these moves, the authorities claiming that not more than 10% of the labourers changed masters and less than 2% left the area altogether, whereas the settlers asserted that 85% of the *serviçaes* abandoned their masters.[53] However, all were agreed that slavery was finally abolished. Redeeming and contracting of slaves from inland ceased, and both automatic recontraction and sub-contracting came to an

[45] AHA, Av–41–76–3, GM to GG 18/12/1903.
[46] Postma, 1897, p. 234.
[47] AHU, 2R–13P, marginal notes on GG to Minister 16/1/1889.
[48] AHU, 1R–23P, Petition to President of Republic 19/11/1910.
[49] Great Britain, 1919, p. 42.
[50] AHU, 1R–23P, GG to Minister 25/1/1914.
[51] Giraúl, 1912, pp. 32–33; Wheeler and Pélissier, 1971, p. 110.
[52] AHU, 1R–23P, *Processo* on abolition of slavery.
[53] Diniz, 1914, pp. 81–83; Viúva Bastos, 1913, p. 13.

end.[54] Furthermore, the length of contracts was reduced to a maximum of two years.[55]

After the abolition of slavery, there were important changes in the nature of the labour force. Some of the *serviçaes* left the south, either to return to their homes of origin or to seek their fortunes in northern Angola. But most of them remained, and with their skills and knowledge of the area, these Kimbari became a stable proletariat. A certain number also managed to set themselves up successfully as independent petty bourgeois producers, or were employed as skilled and supervisory labour.[56] The Ki-Mbundu language, syncretic Afro-European culture, and proletarian class position of the Kimbari population as a whole set them apart from short-term contract workers, who retained rights within African pre-capitalist social formations. However, those local Africans who abandoned their peasant societies and came to settle permanently in centres of employment were generally absorbed into the Kimbari community.[57]

With the revival and expansion of the economy in the 1920s, especially the fishing industry, short-term contract workers from the southern interior began to form the bulk of the labour force. Wages increased from the token payments made under the *servical* system, but they remained very low. Before 1913, the minimum monthly wage for men had been 13p, plus food, clothing, housing and sometimes other benefits.[58] Between 1913 and 1926, this minimum monthly wage increased to between 25p and 40p, according to areas and occupation, whereas the rate for skilled black workers averaged about £1.50. Fringe benefits still seem to have been included, but it is not clear whether these changed in any way.[59]

Low wages accounted for the fact that a considerable amount of coercion continued to characterize the labour process. All natives (*indígenas*) were obliged to undertake a certain yearly period of salaried employment, with a few exceptions, and employers continued to take harsh measures to prevent the escape of their work force.[60] Recruiting was accompanied by a great deal of brutality and flagrant breaches of the law. In 1922, a group of Moçâmedes employers recruited 1,300 labourers in a remote area of northern Angola, using armed sepoys to force chiefs to hand over the requisite number of men.[61] In 1917, it was discovered that

[54] Viúva Bastos, 1913, p. 13; Great Britain, *Parliamentary Papers*, Cd. 7279, Africa 1, 1914, Consul Luanda to Secretary of State for Foreign Affairs, 21/6/1913; AGCSSp, 477–A–IX, Bonnefoux to Propaganda Fide, 3/12/1913; AHM, 14P–31, Relatório do chefe dos serviços de espionagem 31/3/1915.
[55] Lima, 1911, pp. 14–15. [56] Vilela, 1923, pp. 395–397.
[57] Estermann, 1939. [58] Felner, 1940, I, pp. 81–82.
[59] Portugal, 1918, p. 389; Vilela, 1923, pp. 235–241; Galvão, 1930, p. 157.
[60] Portugal, 1918, p. 389; see chapter 3, p. 33.
[61] Guimarães, 1923.

the police in Lubango were arresting 'vagrants', bullying them into signing contracts for São Tomé, and receiving a fee for every man sent.[62] Finally, unpaid forced labour by women on roads appears to have been as common in the south as elsewhere in the Portuguese empire.[63]

Between the workers and the capitalists lay the petty bourgeoisie, a complex and varied class, which shaded off at both ends into the proletariat and the bourgeoisie. The most numerous group consisted of the classic petty bourgeoisie, that is those who owned the means of production but employed little or no labour outside the family unit. The second group, at times overlapping with the first, was made up of employees earning a salary clearly above the level of pauperization. This class was also the most varied in cultural and ethnic terms. Unlike the rest of Angola during this period, the majority of the petty bourgeoisie was made up of whites, but it still included a substantial non-white element. Moreover, both whites and non-whites were divided into Portuguese and Afrikaner communities, differing in terms of language, religion and culture. Altogether, the petty bourgeoisie consisted of several thousand people by the 1920s, although it is impossible to give any accurate statistics.

The classic petty bourgeoisie was to be found in two main areas, the fisheries and the Huíla highlands. In the fisheries, this group developed between the 1860s and the 1890s, when stories of rich fishing banks attracted a current of spontaneous immigration from the Algarve province of southern Portugal. They were poor independent fishermen for the most part, and many of them were illiterate.[64] The rapid alternation of booms and slumps in fishing resulted in a distinct polarization within this group. A few began to buy more boats and to employ significant numbers of *serviçaes*, while many others sank deep into debt with the Moçâmedes traders. The most unfortunate had to sell their boats and were forced to hire boats in return for a proportion of their catches, usually one-third. In some cases, they became salaried employees for the big fisheries, thus moving into the second group within the petty bourgeoisie.[65]

The independent Algarvian fishermen were faced with a certain amount of competition from blacks. The dream of freed slaves was always to set up as independent producers, and they had some success, especially in the ports to the north of Moçâmedes, where the climate was hotter and less healthy and the fishing somewhat poorer.[66] Independent African fishermen were particularly prominent in the coastal settlements of Benguela

[62] Pélissier, 1975, II, p. 947, n. 35. [63] Barns, 1928, p. 151.
[64] Iria, 1942 and 1971.
[65] AHA, Av–41–77–2, Acta da Commissão 11/9/1904, in GM to GG 16/11/1904; Castilho, 1899, pp. 234–235; Vilela, 1923, pp. 175, 285–286, 399 and passim.
[66] Vilela, 1923, pp. 255, 395–397.

province.[67] In the 1890s, enterprising Africans from Cabinda and Luanda also took over some of the transport and trade of dried fish from the whites.[68] The Algarvians fought against this competition by using the colour of their skins. In 1923, a decree was passed whereby all black independent fishermen in the ports to the north of Moçâmedes were to be replaced by whites, on the grounds that the sea was not a 'natural element' for Africans.[69] However, this decree does not appear to have been very effective, for independent African fishermen were mentioned again in subsequent decades.[70]

In the highlands, the classic petty bourgeoisie consisted of small farmers, who often made a living out of transport riding, mercenary service and hunting rather than out of farming proper. In 1881, some 300 Boer trekkers from the Transvaal were given lands in the Huíla highlands by the Portuguese government. They were joined by others of their countrymen, especially during the 1890s, and by 1928 there were about 1,300 Boers in the Huíla and Caconda highlands.[71] In theory, the Boers could receive land grants of up to 1,000 hectares, but in practice land grants were below 100 hectares per family in most cases.[72] Some Boers employed no labour at all outside the family unit and could not send their children to school because they needed them on the land.[73] However, most Boers employed some labour and made a relatively prosperous living out of transport riding.[74] A few, such as Jan Harm Robberts, even became large-scale and wealthy entrepreneurs.[75]

To counter this influx of Boer trekkers, the Portuguese government settled some 1,500 Madeirans in the Huíla highlands between 1884 and 1892.[76] Demobilized soldiers and other immigrants swelled this original group, so that by the late 1920s there were about 4,000 Portuguese whites in the Huíla highlands.[77] The Madeirans were desperately poor small farmers, often illiterate, who were accustomed to intensive irrigated agriculture on tiny plots of land in their native island.[78] They were therefore given little two-hectare plots of irrigable lands along the small streams of the northern Huíla highlands.[79] But neither wheat nor sugar cane were initially successful as cash crops, and the Madeirans lacked the necessary skills for transport riding, mercenary service and hunting.[80] Many of them therefore limited their efforts to producing just enough for

[67] Cid, 1894, p. 38; Azevedo, 1958, p. 405.   [68] Möller, 1974, p. 14.
[69] Matos, 1926, pp. 34–35.   [70] Guimarães and Paiva, 1942, pp. 33–35.
[71] Heese, 1976; Clarence-Smith, 1976b.
[72] *BO*, 27/5/1893, pp. 295–297.
[73] AHU, 2R-22P, Paiva to GM 11/4/1893, in GG to Minister 9/12/1895.
[74] Möller, 1974, p. 17 and passim.   [75] See pp. 52–53.
[76] Nascimento, 1892, passim.   [77] Galvão, 1930, pp. 16–17.
[78] Nascimento, 1892, p. 105; Marvaud, 1912, pp. 186–188.
[79] Portugal, 1918, p. 375.   [80] Felner, 1940, passim.

the subsistence of their families.[81] Others opted for repatriation to Madeira, after the expiry of their initial contracts. Yet others took to trade or entered the inflated local bureaucracy and the church.[82]

However, the local market for wheat and other foodstuffs picked up rapidly in the 1900s and 1910s, largely because of the large-scale military expeditions against the Ovambo and this led to a process of polarization within the Madeiran community. Wheat was an irrigated dry-season crop in the highlands, but by the 1910s all available irrigable land was occupied and the small plots of the Madeirans had already become sub-divided through inheritance. The soil was becoming exhausted because of continuous cultivation and insufficient manuring. Many of the small farmers were deep in debt to commercial houses in Lubango, and some of these indebted farmers were forced off their lands altogether. These landless poor whites became share-croppers or agricultural wage-labourers, in a position which was very similar to that of the poor white fishermen on the coast.[83] Visitors to the highlands were shocked by the sight of these landless, impoverished, illiterate whites, who wore no shoes, were dressed in rags and lived in hovels.[84] However, it would seem that the majority of the Madeirans did not fall to this level, but continued to be petty commodity producers, employing little or no labour outside the family unit.[85]

This particular fraction of the petty bourgeoisie was mainly white, but there were also a few non-whites among them. Two small communities of non-white Afrikaans-speakers were granted lands in the Huíla highlands by the Portuguese authorities. The Makvolk were originally the servants of the Boers, whereas the Rehobother Basters immigrated independently in the early 1880s from South West Africa.[86] Together, these two small communities seem to have numbered only some 250 souls in 1900.[87] They remained in the highlands after the departure of the Boers in 1928 and prospered modestly as small farmers.[88] There were also about 700 Portuguese-speaking *mestiços* or coloureds in the Huíla highlands by the late 1920s,[89] but they were often fully integrated into the Portuguese white community.[90] Local Africans in the highlands did produce a certain amount for the market, but this was generally on communal lands. In 1916, there were only about 400 hectares of land held by *indígenas* in

[81] *C de M*, 28/11/1903, Campos letter.
[82] *J de M*, 1/12/1892 and 21/12/1894; *BG*, XVI, 71, November 1892, p. 647.
[83] Portugal, 1918.   [84] Statham, 1922, pp. 153, 326; Rates, 1929, p. 107.
[85] Barns, 1928, p. 41.
[86] Almeida, 1912, pp. 290, 396 (Makvolk); Paiva, 1938, I, pp. 35, 60–61 (Rehobothers).
[87] Heese, 1976, p. 110. These figures may apply only to the Makvolk.
[88] Medeiros, 1976, pp. 479–480.   [89] Galvão, 1930, pp. 16–17.
[90] Pimentel, 1903, pp. 85–86.

freehold or quasi-freehold tenure in the Huíla highlands.[91] Wheat was the main cash crop on these lands, which may or may not have included the 150 hectares of the christian villagers in the Jau mission.[92] Finally, a few freed slaves were granted small plots of lands in the coastal oases.[93] All in all, the numbers of non-whites in the classic petty bourgeoisie outside fishing was not very great.

The wage-earning fraction of the petty bourgeoisie fell into two groups, those employed in economic functions and those employed by the state. Officials and army officers, who would often combine the two positions, generally stayed in the south for a maximum of three years, especially after the administrative reorganizations of the 1900s.[94] However, a number of settlers were locally recruited for the administration, especially Madeiran settlers who failed to make a living in agriculture.[95] Some officials also married into settler families and remained in the south.[96] Officials were generally badly paid, and most of them resorted to corruption and illegal extortions from African peasants in order to complement their meagre salaries.[97] Nevertheless, officials undoubtedly formed an élite within the petty bourgeoisie.

Supervisory and skilled workers in the fisheries and in other sectors of the economy were generally in a more difficult situation than officials, and it is often hard to draw a precise line between proletarian and petty bourgeois elements in wage employment. Many of the individuals in these positions had originally been independent producers, who had been forced into employment as the result of debt and bankruptcy. Nevertheless, wages in these skilled and supervisory jobs were still much higher than those received by unskilled labourers. In 1909, white foremen in the Baía dos Tigres fisheries were earning about £5 a month, whereas the *serviçaes* only received 19p.[98] In 1917, white ploughmen in the Huíla highlands were paid about £12 a month, whites in other jobs about £3, and unskilled black labourers about 40p.[99] However, these figures may not be strictly comparable, for unskilled labourers received food, clothing and housing in addition to their basic wage, whereas it is not clear if other categories of labour also received these payments in kind.

Non-whites were of some importance in the wage-earning sector of the petty bourgeoisie. *Mestiços* were prominent in the fishing industry, where

[91] Diniz, 1917, p. 6.
[92] Portugal, 1918, pp. 384–385, 448, 468, 477–478.
[93] Nascimento, 1898, p. 91.   [94] AHA, Cod–32–1–33 and 5–5–20.
[95] *Jornal do Commércio*, 14/2/1893, speech by Baracho.
[96] AHA, Av–41–76–3, GM to GG 18/12/1903 for one example; see also Paiva, 1938.
[97] Contreiras, 1894, pp. 29–34; AHA, Cod–32–1–33 and 5–5–20.
[98] AHA, Av–6–1–4, Estatística Industrial 1909.
[99] Portugal, 1918, p. 389 and passim.

they were paid rather less than whites in the early 1920s.[100] Cabindan immigrants and local Kimbari were also employed in skilled and supervisory posts in the fisheries, although it is unfortunately not clear what their wages were.[101] Non-commissioned officers in the army were usually Africans, although their conditions seem to have been poor.[102] In general terms, the numbers of non-whites in the petty bourgeoisie were much smaller than in the colony as a whole. One visitor after the First World War commented on the fact that Moçâmedes did not have the 'trousered blacks', who were such a prominent feature of Luanda and Benguela.[103] The existence of a significant stratum of poor whites in the south had much to do with this anomaly.

The small wandering traders of the interior formed the fraction of the petty bourgeoisie most difficult to analyse, because they straddled capitalist and pre-capitalist social formations. Many small traders were not part of the colonial nucleus at all, such as the Mbali (Mambari) traders of the Caconda highlands and elsewhere. The Mbali held rights in communal lands and left their families or dependants to work these lands, even if they themselves were almost constantly away on long and frequent caravan trips.[104] The ultimate security and self-identification of the Mbali lay in peasant societies, and after the collapse of the rubber boom in the 1910s, most of them became petty commodity producers of maize.[105]

A certain number of white and *mestiço* traders can also be said to have been members of African peasant societies rather than of the colonial nucleus. In the 1860s, the thirteen white and nine *mestiço* traders of Humbe all had African wives, wore African clothes frequently, spoke Lunkhumbi as well if not better than Portuguese, participated in local ceremonies and were entirely subjected to the local chief. It is not clear whether they received lands from the chief, although their wives would presumably have been entitled to land. At any rate, these traders were said to have lost all sense of their racial superiority and to have identified totally with the Africans among whom they lived.[106] This kind of total assimilation into African societies became rarer in later years, as the colonial nucleus grew stronger and more dominating, but it did not cease altogether. In the 1880s, a Portuguese trader set himself up as an independent African chief in the Nkumbi area.[107] And as late as the 1900s, there was an old English trader who lived as an African patriarch in Humbe.[108]

[100] Vilela, 1923, pp. 235–341.
[101] Vilela, 1923, pp. 395–397 (Kimbari); Iria, 1971, pp. 27, 48–49, 68 (Cabindans).
[102] Matos, 1926, pp. 92–94.   [103] Dias, 1923, p. 35.
[104] Childs, 1969, chapter 12; Chatelain, 1918, p. 250.
[105] Pössinger, 1973.   [106] Matta, 1867, p. 276.
[107] AHU, 1R–4P, Capello and Ivens to GG 26/6/1884, in GG to Minister 11/9/1884.   [108] Angebauer, 1927, pp. 124–127.

But the great majority of white and *mestiço* traders were effectively petty bourgeois elements within the colonial nucleus. Most of them were independent traders, owning their own trade goods and therefore akin to the classic petty bourgeoisie, although some were the salaried employees of big commercial concerns.[109] Many were only seasonal traders, who also owned land or other freehold property in the highlands.[110] Others combined trading with other economic activities, such as the Boers, whose trade with Africans was usually subordinate to transport riding and hunting.[111] Full-time traders who were successful often invested their profits in productive activities within the colonial nucleus.[112] Unsuccessful traders fell into debt with the merchants of the colonial nucleus and were in many cases reduced to the position of debt peons.[113] But in spite of frequent economic failures, terrible accidents, harassment at the hands of African chiefs and the general loneliness of life in the bush, petty trading was always an attractive proposition, for it offered a short-cut to success in colonial society.[114] Fantastic profits could be made by the lucky and the persevering, who managed to avoid the great risks and to benefit from the great differences in prices of commodities on the coast and inland.[115]

Above the petty bourgeoisie were the capitalists, who can be divided for analytical purposes into two groups. On the one hand there were those who engaged in productive activities and employed a slave or proletarian labour force which was divorced from the means of production. On the other hand, there were the merchants, who lived partly by servicing the productive sector in the colonial nucleus, but mainly by trade with African peasant societies. Like the small traders, these merchants straddled capitalist and pre-capitalist social formations and derived much of their profit from the petty commodity production of African peasants within pre-capitalist relations of production. Indeed, the distinction between petty bourgeois and bourgeois elements in the trading sector is often hard to make, especially in the absence of detailed statistics on turn-over and profits.

The differences between mercantile capital and productive capital were in practice rather blurred in southern Angola, because capitalists tended to have a finger in every pie, but one can nevertheless distinguish two separate complexes. In the coastal strip, the emphasis was strongly on export-oriented primary production, particularly in the fisheries and cotton plantations, and the major preoccupation of entrepreneurs was with

[109] Portugal, 1903, part e.   [110] Braz, 1918, p. 170.
[111] Statham, 1922, p. 146.   [112] See pp. 49–51.
[113] Duparquet, 1881, p. 569; Galvão, 1944, p. 500.
[114] Almeida, 1912, pp. 529–534.   [115] See chapter 5, pp. 67–68.

the supply of labour. In the highlands, commercial activities were predominant, and the cycle of booms and slumps in commodities produced by African peasants regulated economic life. Problems of security and communications tended to be the main preoccupations of the merchants in the highlands.

The capitalists of southern Angola were a small group, and there was a consistent trend in the direction of the concentration of wealth in fewer and fewer hands. By the turn of the century, three family firms dominated the coastal strip, while the economic activities of the highlands were largely in the hands of three other individuals. By the 1920s, concentration had proceeded still further, and the family of Venancio Guimarães was laying the foundations for an economic domination of southern Angola which was to last until 1975. The history of these various capitalists thus provides the best illustration of the nature and development of a capitalist class in the south. In general terms, it should be noted that investment in a large number of different enterprises was often the key to success.

João Duarte de Almeida's fortune was based on plantations in the coastal oases. Born in 1822, the son of a doctor in a small town of northern Portugal, he came to southern Angola in the 1840s.[116] In 1863, he was responsible for 94% of the cotton exports of Moçâmedes and 24% of those of all Angola.[117] In the 1870s, he was active manufacturing *aguardente* from sugar cane, and lobbying in Lisbon for the abolition of duties on imports of Angolan sugar.[118] At about the same time, he gave his name to a new crop which he had pioneered, *almeidina*, known on the London market as potato-gum rubber.[119] By the mid-1890s, he owned 1,300 hectares of land in the coastal oases, well equipped with a variety of machines and employing about 400 *serviçaes*.[120] In 1896, two years before his death, tax returns show him to have been the second richest man in the province.[121] However, Almeida did not diversify much out of agriculture, and this left his family firm in a very difficult position during the agricultural crisis of the 1900s.[122]

The second major figure in the coastal zone was Seraphim Freire de Figueiredo, who arrived as a penniless immigrant in 1864.[123] He slowly

116 Torres, 1950, pp. 486–487, and photograph; Iria, 1971, p. 81, n. 236.
117 Felner, 1940, III, p. 128.
118 AHU, 48P, Mapa 30/9/1877, in GG to Minister 6/12/1877, and J. D. de Almeida to Minister 4/6/1878.
119 Geraldes and Fragateiro, 1910, p. 73.
120 Nascimento, 1892, p. 32, and 1898, pp. 8–11, 91.
121 AHA, Av–41–71–5, Electoral Register, in GM to GG 4/4/1896; for death, see Torres, 1950, pp. 486–487.
122 AHA, Av–41–78–2, Duarte de Almeida e Companhia to GM 15/2/1910, in GM to GG 18/2/1910.
123 *C de M*, 15/3/1904.

built up his agricultural holdings in the Curoca oasis by ruthlessly exploiting his *serviçaes*,[124] and emerged as the third largest landowner and agricultural producer in the 1900s.[125] But Figueiredo did not make the mistake of putting all his eggs in one basket. In the 1890s, he was actively engaged in commerce and was one of those who specialized in exploiting the Algarvian independent fishermen who had fallen into debt.[126] During the 1900s, he became one of the leading fishing entrepreneurs in the south. In 1904, he was the moving figure in an attempt to set up a marketing cartel in the fishing industry, and he was entrusted with the delicate negotiations aimed at opening up the Mozambique and Transvaal markets to dried fish from southern Angola.[127] In 1915, his family firm of Figueiredo and Almeida took the important step of investing close on £15,000 in the first successful fish-canning factory in the south, the Fabrica Africana, which was also equipped for the production of a much improved quality of dried fish.[128]

Figueiredo was also prominent in the social and political life of the coastal zone. He took a lead in resisting the devastating Nama raids of the 1880s from the Kaokoveld of South West Africa, and became a kind of paramount chief for the indigenous Herero and Khoi peoples of the Curoca oasis area, who brought him their law-suits to settle. He was equally important in settler politics, being often elected to municipal office.[129] He was also renowned for his progressive ideas and belief in science, importing camels from the Canary Islands to improve communications in the Namib desert.[130] The camels were successfully acclimatized and they rendered important services in transporting goods between the Curoca oasis and Moçâmedes.[131] In the same vein, he applied for a monopoly of motorized transport in 1903, and in the following year he imported southern Angola's first motor car.[132]

The richest man in the province, according to the 1896 tax returns, was Manuel José Alves Bastos.[133] A native of the harsh north Portuguese province of Tras-os-Montes, Bastos arrived in Moçâmedes in 1849 with the Portuguese settlers fleeing from xenophobic persecution in Brazil.[134] He began to make his fortune in trade in the 1860s, exploiting the debt-

[124] AHU, 1R, Diversos 1868–1888, GM to DGU 14/6/1880.
[125] AHA, Av–41–62–7, Mapa 1908.
[126] Nascimento, 1898, pp. 14, 54–55; Castilho, 1899, pp. 234–235.
[127] *C de M*, 15/3/1904 and 15/5/1904.
[128] Vilela, 1923, pp. 285 (photograph) and 293; Machado, 1918, pp. 295–296.
[129] *C de M*, 15/3/1904.
[130] Nascimento, 1898, pp. 7, 78.
[131] AHA, Av–41–83–7, GM, Relatório 30/9/1912.
[132] *P em A*, 120, December 1903, p. 694; *C de M*, 21/2/1904.
[133] AHA, Av–41–71–5, Electoral Register, in GM to GG 4/4/1896.
[134] Torres, 1950, photograph opposite p. 342.

ridden fishermen and the petty traders in the interior.[135] By the 1890s, he had acquired major interests in agriculture, fishing and salt production.[136] He died in 1896, and was buried under an ornate mausoleum in the Moçâmedes cemetery.[137]

The leadership of the Bastos family firm then fell to his ambitious son-in-law, Joaquim Cardoso Botelho da Costa, Viscount of Giraúl. Born in northern Portugal, Giraúl made a career as an army doctor in the colonies, receiving his title for services rendered on the 1898 expedition against the Nkhumbi. In 1911, he reached the summit of his professional career when he was appointed director of the health services of Angola and São Tomé. But Giraúl was also pursuing an active business career. He had important investments in central Angola, where he founded and ran the Companhia do Cuanza-Sul, and his greatest coup was marrying the widowed and wealthy daughter of Manuel Bastos in 1895. After Bastos' death in the following year, the family holdings were reorganized in the firm of Viúva Bastos e Filhos, with Giraúl as general manager.[138]

Viúva Bastos e Filhos rapidly became the largest landowner in the coastal strip, controlling 34% of the cultivated area of some 11,000 hectares in 1903 in the coastal oases, and owning other plantations in the foothills.[139] In 1908, the company was responsible for 31% of the legally declared *aguardente* production of Moçâmedes province.[140] This impressive expansion into agriculture was due to a policy of buying up mortgages from the Banco Nacional Ultramarino and seizing the properties of the many planters who went bankrupt during the severe droughts of the 1900s.[141] However, new measures were necessary to face the crisis of the early 1910s, which was due to the suppression of *aguardente* production, the low price of cotton, and the abolition of quasi-slavery. Giraúl therefore created a new entity, the Companhia do Sul de Angola, which incorporated Viúva Bastos and several other firms or individuals.[142] This company was also prominent in fishing during the 1920s, controlling most of the local salt production and investing heavily in tinned fish and fish meal.[143]

Economic life in the highlands tended to be dominated by foreign traders and entrepreneurs with strong South African connections after the 1880s, and William James Chapman was the most influential individual amongst

---

[135] Iria, 1971, p. 38, n. 83; Felner, 1940, I, p. 79; Duparquet, 1953, p. 163.
[136] Nascimento, 1892, pp. 32, 36; Iria, 1971, p. 66; Vilela, 1923, p. 346.
[137] Torres, 1950, photograph opposite p. 342.
[138] *Grande Enciclopédia Portuguesa e Brasileira*, XII, pp. 409–410.
[139] *C de M*, 16/11/1903.   [140] AHA, Av–41–62–7, Mapa 1908.
[141] Viúva Bastos, 1913, pp. 16–17; AHA, Av–41–92–1, CG to GG 18/3/1905.
[142] *Grande Enciclopédia Portuguesa e Brasileira*, XII, pp. 409–410.
[143] Vilela, 1923, p. 326; Rates, 1929, p. 63.

them. Chapman was the son of the famous explorer of southern Africa, and he began his career as an elephant hunter and ivory trader in South West Africa in 1874. Together with a small group of South West African hunter–traders, he moved to southern Angola in the early 1880s, when ivory supplies close to Damaraland had become exhausted and the Herero–Nama war was making the whole region unsafe for trade. When supplies of ivory also ran out in southern Angola, Chapman switched first to the cattle trade with Ovamboland and then in the 1900s to the rubber trade in south-east Angola.[144] Although primarily a trader, Chapman was also active in transport riding, road building, wagon supplying, cattle ranching and gold prospecting.[145]

Chapman was an English South African by birth and upbringing, but he became a leading member of the Boer community in southern Angola, marrying an Afrikaner girl and joining the Dutch Reformed Church.[146] His 200-hectare farm was in the district of Humpata, which served as a kind of unofficial capital for all the Angola Boers.[147] Nevertheless, Chapman retained various English connections, being one of the sources of information for the British Foreign Office on military campaigns in southern Angola.[148] From the 1910s, he also attempted to persuade the Angola Boers to claim British nationality, in order to resist the increasing pressures of the Portuguese administration.[149] In 1928, he left Angola with the Boers for South West Africa, where he died four years later.[150]

The second major figure in the highlands was an Afrikaner, Jan Harm Robberts, who trekked out of the Transvaal in 1877.[151] He was the largest landowner in the highlands, with 800 hectares in 1893, and engaged in transport riding, mercenary service, fruit farming and gold prospecting.[152] But the basis of Robberts' success lay in his ivory business, in which he employed about a dozen professional hunters and an unknown number of auxiliary personnel.[153] In the early 1890s, he went to the Transvaal to persuade Boer hunters who had lost their livelihood to trek to Angola.[154] He provided his hunters with wagons, horses, rifles and ammunition, and in return received a large share of the ivory which they

---

[144] Tabler, 1973, pp. 21–25; Stals, 1968, pp. 305–307, 317–318.
[145] Heese, 1976, pp. 106–107 (transport); Paiva, 1938, II, pp. 229–232 (cattle); *J de M*, 15/5/1892 and 1/12/1892 (road and gold).
[146] Tabler, 1973, p. 24; Gibson, 1905, p. 120.
[147] AHMH, 12, Processo de Mediação 1899.
[148] NAZ, BS2/104, Chapman to Stevens 22/2/1905.
[149] AHU, 2R–22P, GG to Minister 29/11/1918.
[150] Tabler, 1973, p. 25.   [151] Postma, 1897, p. 29.
[152] *BO*, 27/5/1893 (lands); Heese, 1976, p. 107 (transport); AHU, 4R–2P, Captain Dragoons to GM 2/8/1901, in GG to Minister 25/11/1901 (mercenary); Gibson, 1905, p. 122 (fruit); AHA, Av–31–7–5, GH to GG 17/5/1902 (gold).
[153] *Le Philafricain*, II, 2, p. 42.
[154] Hattingh, 1975, pp. 307–313.

obtained. He made such profits from this business that he bought several farms in the Transvaal and finally left Angola altogether.[155]

The last leading capitalist in the highlands was not a foreigner, but a *mestiço* trader from Caconda, António José de Almeida, who made his fortune originally in the ivory and cattle trade of Ovamboland in the 1870s.[156] He maintained his interests in the cattle trade of this area and later spread them to Barotseland.[157] But the real basis of his prosperity lay in the rubber trade of south-east Angola. By the 1900s, Almeida had the most extensive network of rubber trading houses in southern Angola,[158] and in the 1890s he was busy opening up trade routes in north-eastern Angola.[159] In 1899, tax returns show him to have been the richest man in the Huíla district, although unfortunately there are no figures for the Humpata district, which might serve to compare his wealth with that of Chapman and Robberts.[160] Almeida was the trader of the highlands who diversified most out of commerce. Apart from transport riding, mercenary service, gold prospecting and cattle ranching,[161] Almeida also had large plantations for wheat and sugar cane in the highlands and in the foothills.[162]

Concentration of capital increased still further in the south after the economic crisis of the 1910s, and in the following decade a new figure rose to prominence, Venancio Guimarães. His origins remain obscure, but by the early 1920s he was already involved in cotton growing and cattle ranching on a large scale in the foothills.[163] By the late 1920s, he had become the largest cotton producer in the whole colony.[164] In later years, the family firm of Venancio Guimarães Sobrinho exerted an extraordinary degree of economic, social and political power in southern Angola, and Guimarães came to be known as the *cacique* or political boss of the south.[165] The 'reign' of Guimarães was broken only by the Angolan civil war, during which the family fled the country, apparently to Brazil.[166]

These brief and incomplete life histories to a large extent speak for themselves, but it is worth stressing the importance of political power and influence in the economic life of the south. Access to state power was

---

[155] Heese, 1976, pp. 106–107.   [156] Duparquet, 1953, pp. 163–165.
[157] Möller, 1974, p. 60; NAZ, KDE/2/35/2, Alves to Lewanika 20/8/1908.
[158] Portugal, 1903, part e.   [159] Pélissier, 1975, I, p. 359.
[160] AHA, Av–41–73–1, Electoral Register, in GM to GG 18/9/1899.
[161] Pimentel, 1903, pp. 25–26 (transport); AHU, 4R–2P, Lieutenant Dragoons to GM 6/8/1901, in GG to Minister 25/11/1901 (mercenary); *J de M*, 1/12/1892 (gold); Braz, 1918, p. 140 (cattle).
[162] Nascimento, 1892, p. 116; *C de M*, 16/11/1903.
[163] Guimarães, 1923, p. 46.
[164] Galvão, 1930, p. 178; Rates, 1929, p. 96.
[165] Medeiros, 1976, pp. 594–595; personal communication Lubango 1973.
[166] *Angola Solidarity Committee News*, 13, October 1976, p. 6.

fundamental for the whole labour question, firstly in maintaining the system of slavery for nearly forty years after its official abolition, and then in extracting migrant labour from African peasant societies on terms as advantageous as possible. The state was also the guarantor of security in the interior for traders, and it provided one of the biggest markets for commerce and other service industries. From a negative point of view, official legislation brought ruin to the *aguardente* producers in the 1900s and 1910s, and the refusal of the government to build a railway in the 1880s and 1890s led to the frustration of many hopes.[167] In short, the southern capitalists were in very much the same position as that analysed by Helmut Bley for South West Africa.[168] They exercised remarkable power within the colonial nucleus, but remained in a situation of abject dependence on the colonial state.

The formal avenue to influencing the colonial state lay in elections to the Portuguese parliament, but these were generally of little real importance. Angola only disposed of one or two seats in the *cortes*, and the administration manipulated the thousands of Ambaquista and Mbali votes to ensure the success of the official candidates.[169] The only free and serious elections seem to have been those held in 1911, just after the republican revolution. The provinces of Moçâmedes and Huíla formed a constituency on their own, the franchise was reformed and extended, and the left-wing Reformista candidate carried the day by obtaining the votes of the poor whites in the highlands.[170]

Local elections for the Moçâmedes town council were of greater significance. This town council was set up in 1855,[171] and it enjoyed a fair amount of revenue from local taxes, property and government subsidies. Within the political traditions of Latin Europe, the town council functioned as the representative organ of settler opinion, in the absence of a legislative council.[172] The settlers called for some kind of political reform on South African lines, which would have given them more local autonomy, but the authorities did not respond.[173] In the 1920s, the republican régime conceded a certain measure of administrative decentralization, but this only led to the concentration of dictatorial powers in the hands of the High Commissioners and not to a representative government elected by settlers.[174]

The settlers were therefore reduced to informal political activities, which flourished in a climate of freedom of expression and were aimed at rallying public opinion in the metropolis. Between 1881 and 1926, twenty-

[167] All issues treated in detail by settler press.   [168] Bley, 1971.
[169] AHU, 1R–16P, GG to Minister 29/2/1896 and 14/5/1896.
[170] *O Sul*, 22/5/1911 and 23/7/1911.   [171] Milheiros, 1972, pp. 202–203.
[172] AHU, 1R–16P, GG to Minister 14/5/1896.
[173] *C de M*, 1/10/1903.   [174] Wheeler and Pélissier, 1971, pp. 113–115.

four different newspapers appeared in Moçâmedes and Lubango. Many of these were only ephemeral publications, but the *Jornal de Mossamedes* was the most important newspaper published in the colony outside Luanda. It appeared fairly regularly every fortnight from 1881 to 1895, printed on its own press and running to four closely-packed pages.[175] Pamphlets, petitions and law-suits were also frequently employed by the settlers to appeal to Luanda or Lisbon over the heads of the authorities.[176]

Three men stood out in this long struggle to influence state power, with the *Jornal de Mossamedes* as their principal weapon for many years.[177] Rodolpho de Santa Brigida e Sousa was the parish priest of Moçâmedes, possibly of Goanese origin, and a stout defender of the settler's labour policies.[178] Vital de Bettencourt do Canto was a retired army captain, who had married a wealthy widow with plantations in the foothills, and who had a reputation for treating his *serviçaes* like animals.[179] Antonio Corrêa Mendes was the local chemist, and a plantation owner of some importance.[180] However, it would seem that the settlers lost rather than gained in political influence over the years, and the ruthless policies of Norton de Matos in the 1920s set the scene for the long repression of any criticism of the authorities under Salazar.[181]

From the settler press, petitions and pamphlets, and from other scattered evidence, there emerges a fairly well-defined and consistent set of ideological positions. At the level of the capitalists, there existed a very Victorian outlook. Hard work, honesty and thrift were the virtues which they proclaimed, and they fervently embraced a belief in the sanctity of progress, profit and private property. Religion and patriotism were supported as the principles of social order, and class attitudes were pronounced, especially the belief that the poor were poor because of moral depravity. The very portraits of the founding fathers of Moçâmedes exude an atmosphere of confidence and self-righteousness so typical of Victorian capitalism.[182]

A more general and pervasive ideological phenomenon was the existence of a virulent form of racism, for which Moçâmedes was famous in Angola as early as 1880.[183] Moçâmedes was the only town in the colony in the 1890s in which racial discrimination prevailed in schools, and in the 1910s residential segregation was more clearly marked than in any

175 Lopo, 1964, pp. 58–59, 88–90, 108.
176 AHU, 1R–14P, GG to Minister 12/1/1899.
177 AHA, Av–41–71–3, GM to GG 30/8/1894.
178 Torres, 1950, photograph opposite p. 210; Sousa, 1887.
179 AHU, 2R–9P, GG to Minister 17/4/1885.
180 AHA, Av–41–71–3, GM to GG 30/8/1894; Nascimento, 1892, p. 32.
181 Wheeler and Pélissier, 1971, pp. 113–115.
182 Torres, 1950 and Alves, 1970 provide good examples.
183 AHU, 2R–4P, CG to Minister 14/9/1880.

other major town in the colony.[184] The Boers were also famous for their extreme views on the racial question. In 1908, the great majority of the Afrikaners in the Huíla highlands quarrelled violently with the minister of the Dutch Reformed Church, who had had the audacity to say that the same minister should serve both the white and the coloured congregations of the church.[185] However, racial attitudes appear to have been less marked in the Portuguese community of the highlands, especially with regard to *mestiços*.[186]

All the usual racist clichés were put forward by the Moçâmedes settlers in their attempts to justify their racial prejudices. They alleged that only blacks could engage in hard physical labour in the tropics and that corporal punishment was essential to make them work properly.[187] The negro race was portrayed as lazy, childish and incapable of solving complex problems, because it was judged to be on an inferior rung on the ladder of biological evolution.[188] At the same time, the settlers tried to project an image of kindly paternalist whites, weighed down by cares in their efforts to ensure the happiness of their improvident black wards.[189]

In addition to the fundamental cleavage between whites and blacks, there was a fairly strong element of ethnic opposition between different groups of whites. This was most clearly seen in the antagonism between Portuguese and Afrikaners, which occasionally degenerated into violent incidents.[190] However, there was also a certain amount of friction between Portuguese of different origins. In particular, the north Portuguese independent immigrants tended to consider themselves very superior to the state-subsidized Madeiran immigrants.[191] Finally, it should be noted that ethnic splits could at times override the fundamental racial cleavage. Thus in 1893, the Portuguese feared that all the Afrikaans-speakers, both white and coloured, might rise up in rebellion against the Portuguese.[192]

The racism of the petty bourgeoisie appears to have stemmed from a profound sense of insecurity. Independent fishermen, small farmers, petty traders and the like were constantly threatened by impoverishment and proletarianization. They were at the mercy of natural disasters and social calamities and were often incapable of breaking out of the vicious circle of debt. It can thus be argued that racial and ethnic discrimination was

184 Contreiras, 1894, p. 87, n. 1; Dias, 1923, p. 35.
185 Van der Merwe, 1951, pp. 22–41.
186 Nascimento, 1892, pp. 57–58; Medeiros, 1976, passim.
187 *J de M*, 20/7/1884; *Commercio de Mossamedes*, 14/2/1909; Giraúl, 1912, pp. 19–20.
188 Sousa, 1887, pp. 399, 403; AHA, Av–41–90–6, Petition 6/9/1904.
189 Giraúl, 1912.
190 *J de M*, 5/11/1894.
191 AHU, 1R–12P, GG to Minister 28/4/1892.
192 AHU, 2R–17P, Paiva to GG 3/3/1893, in GG to Minister 11/4/1893.

just one of the ways in which sections of the petty bourgeoisie attempted to maximize their own security at the expense of others.

The racism of the capitalists was a little more complex, for non-whites were less expensive to employ than whites in many cases, and non-whites could often produce commodities more cheaply than whites. But racism was a useful tool of social control over the bulk of the labour force, and was especially useful in the long struggle of the entrepreneurs to perpetuate a system of slavery in the fisheries and plantations. Furthermore, racism was a way of winning over petty bourgeois elements who were shamelessly exploited by the capitalists and who might have constituted a considerable political threat.

Finally, one has to place the colonial nucleus within the wider context of southern Angola as a whole. White settlers were not only threatened by black labourers and black competitors within colonial society, but also by the menace of the African peasant masses beyond the confines of the colonial nucleus. This problem was particularly great during the period of the military subjugation of peasant societies, when raids were a constant feature of life in the colonial nucleus. It is therefore possible to argue that the particularly fierce resistance of the African peasants of southern Angola also contributed to the strong racism of the southern whites. It is interesting to note in this context that the Moçâmedes settlers decided to call on Queen Victoria for protection in 1878, both because of the abolition of slavery and because the authorities were incapable of protecting plantation owners from bandit raids.[193]

193 Almeida, 1880, pp. 27–28.

5

The peasant economy

There are about as many definitions of a peasant as there are authors who use the word, so that it is necessary to begin by clarifying the sense in which it is employed here. For the purposes of this book, a peasant is defined as a rural dweller who functions essentially within pre-capitalist relations of production, but is to a certain extent dependent on the capitalist commodity or labour markets. It is thus a fluid and transitional category, and an attempt will be made to define more closely the nature of the articulation between capitalist and pre-capitalist modes of production in this and in the subsequent chapter. Suffice it to say here that African tributary societies in southern Angola, in contrast to the colonial nucleus, were characterized by the communal ownership of the means of production, kinship systems of apportioning labour power, and the relative unimportance of production for the market.

Pastoralism was the dominant branch of production within African societies during this period, and more particularly cattle rearing. Cattle provided a large proportion of subsistence requirements, as well as manure and hides. Cattle also constituted the chief kind of capital investment, were important as currency and were a major article of both internal and external trade. The flood plains and the medium altitude areas around the highlands formed the best cattle country, with abundant sweet veld pastures and adequate water supplies. Lack of water and poor pastures inhibited pastoralism in the coastal Namib desert and in the Kalahari sands of south-eastern Angola. Nor were the highlands particularly suited to cattle raising, for abundant rains created sour veld grazing and encouraged the spread of diseases.[1]

Pastoralism was extensive in nature and marked by few or no technical innovations before the 1960s. Patterns of transhumance were complex and shifting, following palatable grasses and supplies of water. The concentration of large herds at water points in the dry season and the kraaling of

[1] Urquhart, 1963, p. 104 and passim; Estermann, 1964, pp. 53–56.

58

cattle at night were the main causes of the rapid spread of epizootics, which devastated herds at fairly frequent intervals. The quality of cattle was poor, as resistance to difficult local conditions was more important than high yields of milk or meat, and few or no attempts at cross-breeding were made until the 1960s.[2]

Although cattle were always important in local trade between and within African societies, they did not at first attract much interest from colonial traders. Many of the traders from the colonial nucleus did deal in cattle on a fairly extensive scale, but chiefly as an intermediary commodity with which to purchase ivory.[3] Nevertheless, Moçâmedes exported a few hides and sold live cattle or salt beef to St Helena and to passing ships in the period up to the 1880s.[4] Similarly, South West African traders bought a few cattle in Ovamboland, probably for export to St Helena or overland to the Cape.[5]

The limited export trade in cattle suddenly intensified from the late 1880s. The cocoa boom in São Tomé and Principe turned these two islands into a major market for live cattle from Moçâmedes.[6] At the same time, the growth of plantations and the needs of European military expeditions provided neighbouring markets in the Congo estuary, Gabon and Dahomey.[7] Exports of live cattle from Moçâmedes reached a peak value of nearly £5,000 in 1897 at the comparatively low average price of £3.30 per head.[8] Prices rose steadily during the following decade to reach a maximum of £10.40 per head in 1907, but the value of exports from Moçâmedes fell sharply.[9] This was due firstly to the great rinderpest epizootic of 1897–1899, which in many areas destroyed over 90% of all cattle.[10] It was also due to the prolonged drought of the 1900s, which made it virtually impossible to drive large herds of cattle across the Namib desert to Moçâmedes.[11] Much of the remaining cattle trade of the southern interior was thus diverted to Benguela, where prices remained well below those obtaining in Moçâmedes.[12]

Another major market for cattle from southern Angola grew up in South Africa from the late 1880s. Prices of meat and transport oxen

[2] Estermann, 1964, pp. 53–56; Carvalho and Silva, 1973; Teixeira, 1934, pp. 665–671.
[3] McKiernan, 1954, pp. 107–108; Magyar, 1859, pp. 298–299.
[4] Silva, 1971–1973, 33, p. 254; Delgado, 1944, II, pp. 59–61.
[5] Stals, 1968, p. 305; Moorsom, 1973, p. 31.
[6] Almeida, 1912, pp. 562–563; Gomes, 1894, p. 117.
[7] *J de M*, 1/10/1893.   [8] *Estatística Commercial*, 1909, p. xv.
[9] *Estatística Commercial*, 1909, p. xv; see graphs.
[10] Paiva, 1938, II, pp. 99–104; AGCSSp, 477–A–VIII, Antunes to Propagation de la Foi 22/11/1898.
[11] Clarence-Smith, 1974; AHMH, 8, GH to GM 18/6/1902.
[12] *Estatística Commercial*, 1909, p. xv; Braz, 1918, p. 141.

soared in South Africa owing to the mining revolution, and it became profitable to import cheap cattle on the hoof from southern Angola, in spite of the long and difficult trek across the Kalahari.[13] An added attraction was that cattle did not have to pay the Portuguese export duty of about £1 per head which was levied on the coast.[14] As this was officially contraband trade, no record was kept of the numbers of cattle exported by this route, but it is clear that many thousands of cattle were sent to South Africa from southern Angola during the 1890s.[15]

But the South African market did not survive the rinderpest epizootic. Traders found a better source of supply in Barotseland, which was miraculously spared rinderpest.[16] In addition, both the British and the German governments set up much tighter controls over the overland trade route, mainly in order to prevent the acquisition of firearms by African societies.[17] The cattle trade was thus reoriented towards Benguela, where corruption in matters affecting the firearms trade was rampant and imports of trade arms were legal.[18] By 1906, the Kalahari trade route had fallen into disuse.[19]

During the 1910s and 1920s, the trade in cattle changed in nature and increased in scale. Exports of live cattle to regional African markets were largely replaced by exports of hides to metropolitan Portugal. Between 1913 and 1926, hides became the second most valuable export of Moçâmedes after fish and whale products, with an average annual export value of about £15,000.[20] Some of the hides of southern Angola also went through Benguela, and live cattle were still exported on a small scale to São Tomé, Fernando Poo, the Congo estuary and Katanga.[21] Cattle had become established as the greatest source of wealth in the interior of southern Angola.

Crop cultivation formed the second major branch of production for African societies, but it was almost entirely confined to providing for subsistence needs. Maize was the staple crop in the highlands and millet in the flood plains. Yields were low, consequent on the use of shifting hoe cultivation on poor and drought-prone soils, with a minimum of manuring or irrigation. The area under cultivation was also very restricted, being

[13] Wilson and Thompson, 1971, II, chapter 1; Tabler, 1973, p. 39.
[14] AHU, 2R–17P, GG to Minister 9/11/1893.
[15] AHU, Companhia de Moçâmedes, 9, Chefe Humbe to GM 5/1/1896; Tabler, 1973, p. 39.
[16] *Journal des Missions Evangéliques*, LXXVII, 1902, I, p. 378.
[17] Nitsche, 1913, p. 147, for Germans; Livingstone Museum Manuscript Collection, G/19/6, Journal of F. Worthington 1902, for British.
[18] Almeida, 1912, pp. 537–543; Braz, 1918, p. 141.
[19] Seiner, 1909, p. 106.
[20] *Estatística Commercial*, various years; see graphs.
[21] Teixeira, 1934, pp. 665–671.

limited by lack of water, sandy or rocky soils and the prevalence of winter frosts.[22] Southern Angola was little suited to agriculture and severe droughts led to tens of thousands dying of starvation, as in the disastrous years 1915–1916.[23]

Trade in crops was on a very small scale, both between African societies and with the colonial nucleus. Tobacco was grown in the northern part of the area and was used extensively for local trade, but did not become an export crop.[24] Maize was grown as a cash crop in the highlands, but almost exclusively for the very limited market within the colonial nucleus.[25] A sizeable export trade in maize did not develop until the widening and extension of the Moçâmedes railway in the 1960s, although the arrival of the light railway at Lubango in 1923 did something to stimulate it.[26] Africans also grew a little wheat in the highlands, but they found it difficult to compete with the settlers who had seized almost all the land suitable for irrigated agriculture.[27]

A brief mention should also be made of mining and crafts. Iron ore from the area of the present Cassinga mines and copper ore from the region of the Otavi–Tsumeb mining complex were used by the Ovambo and Nkhumbi for the manufacture and trade of a multitude of metal artefacts. Together with salt from the Etosha Pan area, these metal objects were the staple products of local trade.[28] Clay pots, reed mats, wooden bowls and a variety of ornaments were also produced and traded locally.[29] However, none of these products ever entered the export sector and large-scale mining was monopolized by the colonial nuclei of southern Angola and South West Africa respectively.

Hunting and fishing constituted another major branch of production, although ethnographic texts tend to play down the role of hunting in view of the present scarcity of game. In the nineteenth century, however, game was still a very important part of the diet of indigenous societies, probably far more important than meat from domestic animals.[30] Dried fish and game meat were articles of local trade, in addition to various types of ornaments derived from the products of the hunt.[31] Hunting also provided extremely valuable commodities for trade with the outside world, especially ivory, but also ostrich feathers, rhinoceros horn and a variety

[22] Urquhart, 1963.
[23] AGCSSp, 478–A–VI, Bonnefoux to TRP 20/8/1916.
[24] Delachaux, 1948, p. 75.   [25] Heese, 1976, pp. 87–88.
[26] Teixeira, 1934, pp. 501, 651; Mendes, 1958, pp. 22–23.
[27] Portugal, 1918, pp. 384–385, 448, 468, 477–478 and passim.
[28] Brochado, 1855, pp. 194–195; Andersson, 1875, pp. 225, 235, 315; McKiernan, 1954, pp. 102–103.
[29] Urquhart, 1963, pp. 127–128.
[30] Estermann, 1964, p. 56; Loeb, 1962, p. 314; Lima, 1977, pp. 91–92.
[31] Möller, 1974, pp. 53 and passim; Tönjes, 1911, 84–85; Carvalho, 1904, p. 41.

of skins.[32] Southern Angola's vast semi-arid spaces were well provided with game, and its ivory was of the most highly prized variety to be found in dry savanna country.[33]

Techniques of hunting were revolutionized in the second half of the nineteenth century by the introduction of much more efficient firearms,[34] and this coincided with the growing demand for ivory in the West. The abolition of the royal monopoly over ivory in 1834 was also a powerful local stimulus to hunting in Angola, especially during the economic crisis consequent on the abolition of the Atlantic slave trade.[35] Indeed, Moçâmedes was originally founded in 1840 as a coastal factory to intensify the extraction of ivory from the southern marches of the colony.[36]

The ivory boom lasted from the 1840s to the 1880s in southern Angola, but at the expense of the near extermination of elephants in the region. Ivory was most important in the exports of Moçâmedes in the early 1850s. In 1854, £4,300 worth was exported through the port and it was by far the most valuable commodity.[37] But as the elephant frontier retreated rapidly towards south-eastern Angola, Moçâmedes traders were squeezed out of the trade by their rivals from Benguela and Walvis Bay.[38] Moreover, African hunters were progressively displaced during the 1870s by the white hunter–traders of South West Africa, who had the advantages of modern rifles, horses and ox-wagons.[39] The brief revival of ivory exports from Moçâmedes in the early 1880s was thus mainly due to the migration of these hunter–traders into southern Angola.[40] From then on, hunting fell increasingly into the hands of agents of the colonial nucleus, and some Africans were reduced to bartering grain for game meat.[41]

Closely linked to hunting were various forms of gathering or collecting. Roots, honey, wild fruit and other bush foods constituted an appreciable supplement to the diet of African societies.[42] In addition, collecting provided a number of commodities for consumption and trading purposes, such as red dye-wood, ostrich egg-shells, cannabis, arrow poison, beeswax and rubber.[43] The last two of these collected goods assumed special importance as major export products.

[32] Torres, 1950, pp. 435–466; *BO*, 43, 26/10/1885.
[33] White, 1892.
[34] *Chamber's Encyclopaedia*, 1968, V, pp. 646–648.
[35] Munro, 1976, pp. 51–52; Delgado, 1940, pp. 111–112 for date, which appears as 1836 in Munro.
[36] Delgado, 1940, p. 119.   [37] Felner, 1940, II, pp. 264–265.
[38] AHU, 1R Diversos 1868–1888, GM Relatório 1877, for Benguela; Palgrave, 1969, pp. 47–48, for Walvis Bay.
[39] Stals, 1968, pp. 304–306.   [40] See chapter 3, p. 52.
[41] Pimentel, 1903, p. 81; Carvalho, 1904, p. 41.
[42] Loeb, 1962, p 314.
[43] Brochado, 1855, pp. 195, 204–207; Andersson, 1856, pp. 203–205; Hahn, 1867, p. 291.

The rubber boom in southern Angola began in about 1885, when it was discovered that the roots of a shrub called *carpodinus gracilis* produced an inferior but abundant kind of latex, which could profitably be sold on the expanding world market. This shrub grew only in deep well-drained sands, receiving moderate rainfall, and it was thus found in the greatest quantities in the northern parts of the Kalahari sandveld of south-eastern Angola.[44] Production was largely in the hands of recent Cokwe and Luvale immigrants, who reduced the roots to a pulp and then used a variety of rudimentary techniques to purify the latex.[45] Attempts were made to leave enough of the roots in the ground to secure the eventual regeneration of the shrub, but it would seem that the destruction of *carpodinus gracilis* was proceeding apace under the pressure of over-intensive exploitation. The main production areas thus tended to shift steadily further eastwards.[46]

The major rubber-producing areas were far from Moçâmedes and within the traditional trading sphere of Beneguela, so that southern merchants were only very partially successful in their attempts to cash in on this new boom. In the period 1890–1895, Moçâmedes accounted for only 0.4% of Angola's rubber exports,[47] and in 1903, one of the peak years for southern exports, this figure still stood at only 3%.[48] But rubber was nevertheless very important to the economy of the poor southern marches of the colony, becoming Moçâmedes' second export by value during the 1900s with an average annual return of about £13,500.[49] It should also be remembered that a large proportion of the rubber exports of northern and central Angola came not from root rubber but from creepers and trees which did not grow in the south.[50]

The profitability of the collection of wild rubber was increasingly threatened by falling prices on the world market, due to the expansion of plantation production in South East Asia during the 1900s.[51] In 1913, a crisis point was reached. Prices collapsed and the rubber boom came to a rapid close.[52] African rubber collectors in south-eastern Angola thus found themselves in a very difficult situation, which was only partially compensated by switching over to the collection of wax.[53]

Wax had for long been a minor product in the exports of southern Angola. In the 1840s and 1850s, it had come from the highlands.[54] But in

[44] Geraldes and Fragateiro, 1910; FO, *AS*, 4391, 1908; Hobson, 1960, p. 2.
[45] Gibbons, 1904, I, pp. 240–242; NAZ, BS2/160, Harding Report 4/7/1900.
[46] FO, *AS*, 4391, 1908; Couceiro, 1910, pp. 278–282.
[47] Portugal, 1897, pp. 71–72.   [48] *BO*, 1905, Apenso 20.
[49] See graphs.   [50] Geraldes and Fragateiro, 1910.
[51] Couceiro, 1910, pp. 277–278.
[52] AGCSSp, 476–B–V, Goepp to TRP 7/7/1915; Meyer, 1918, p. 38; Harms, 1975.
[53] AHM, 15P–16, Relatório da Rebelião dos Luchazes, 1917; Vellut, 1977, p. 303.
[54] Brochado, 1855, pp. 204–207.

the 1920s, wax seems to have been almost exclusively a product of eastern Angola. There was no construction of hives, wax being collected by setting fire to the bush in order to raid the hives of the wild bees.[55] But wax could not really replace rubber as an export commodity, and even in a good year such as 1926, the total wax exports of Moçâmedes came to only £3,500.[56]

Related to hunting and collecting was slave raiding, although this was not strictly speaking a productive activity. A certain number of slaves were generated from within the various societies, but the majority seem to have been captives of war.[57] The people most subjected to raiding were the decentralized Ngangela and Wiko peoples, and the main predators were the Ovambo, the Cokwe and the Luvale.[58] The Ovimbundu, who had been great slave raiders in the days of the Atlantic slave trade, now confined themselves to the business of buying slaves to sell to the colonial nucleus, and the small southern Ovimbundu tribes became a prey to Ovambo and Cokwe raids.[59]

The trade in slaves, which had declined drastically in the 1840s as a result of the suppression of the Atlantic slave trade, recovered slowly with the development of plantations and fisheries in the colonial nucleus. In particular, the cocoa boom in São Tomé from the late 1880s led to a great resurgence in the trade. Exports of *serviçaes* to São Tomé averaged 2,500 a year between 1887 and 1897 and 4,000 a year during the ensuing decade.[60] Southern Angola was involved in this new spurt of slave exports, but it is impossible to even guess at the proportional importance of the south, as the trade was entirely conducted through Caconda and Benguela.[61] Slave exports were also linked to the ivory and rubber trades, as slave porters were often used to carry merchandise to the coast.[62] This traffic in human beings was energetically repressed by the new republican authorities after 1910 and was more or less stamped out within a few years.[63] The end of slave exports thus coincided closely with the collapse of the rubber boom.

The goods acquired by African tributary societies from the capitalist

[55] Teixeira, 1934, pp. 674–677.
[56] *Estatística Commercial*, 1926; Vellut, 1977, p. 303, for comparative prices paid to producer.
[57] Nogueira, 1880, p. 104.
[58] Estermann, 1956–1961, I, pp. 141–146 for Ovambo raiding; *Le Philafricain*, I, 7, p. 3, for Cokwe raiding; NAZ, BS2/159, Harding Report 4/7/1900, for Luvale raiding.
[59] Childs, 1969, chapter 12; *Le Philafricain* and Chatelain, 1918, passim.
[60] Roçadas, 1914, p. 33.
[61] AHA, Av-41-66-7, GM to GG 27/12/1894.
[62] NAZ, BS2/159, Bricker to Harding 27/2/1900.
[63] AGCSSp, 477-A-X, Bonnefoux to Propaganda Fide 3/12/1913.

world in return for their commodities can be divided into consumer and producer goods, firearms being the most important item in the latter category. Firearms were particularly vital for peoples who depended heavily on hunting and raiding, such as the Cokwe and Ovambo.[64] Horses were also imported on a small scale for use in hunting and raiding, and some of the Ovambo became expert riders.[65] However, horses were not adapted to local climatic conditions and even 'salted' horses, supposedly immune to horse sickness, died very easily.[66]

Alcoholic beverages, cloth and beads were the main consumer goods imported by African societies, although neither of the last two items assumed the importance which they sometimes did in other parts of Africa. Alcohol was thus the chief consumer import, although one should perhaps call it a 'destroyer good' in view of its negative effects on productivity. In 1898, one of the chiefs of the Huíla highlands complained bitterly that his people bartered cattle and grain for *aguardente* and became half-starved besotted drunkards as a result.[67] The powerful Ovambo chiefs were also aware of the ravages caused by the imports of strong alcoholic spirits, and they made attempts to prevent the consumption of imported alcohol by commoners.[68]

The organization of exchange in the interior of southern Angola was simple. There were no fixed markets, and local trade was conducted by individuals or small parties moving from one homestead to another hawking their wares.[69] However, powerful chiefs exercised a monopoly over long-distance trade, so that royal kraals functioned as markets of a kind.[70] Cattle, cloth, beads or tobacco were used as currency,[71] and when European money began to circulate, British and German coins were preferred to Portuguese paper notes.[72]

Mobile trade was the rule for much of this period, as fixed stores were generally to be found only within the colonial nucleus. Only at the height of certain booms would fixed stores appear in the African tributary societies most affected, such as in Ovamboland in the 1870s during the ivory boom, or in south-east Angola in the 1900s during the rubber boom.[73] African traders would therefore band together in caravans and make trading expeditions to their neighbours or to the towns and ports of the colonial nucleus. The Mbali (Mambari) of the Caconda and central highlands were especially prominent in this caravan trade in southern

[64] Couceiro, 1910, pp. 80–87.   [65] Capello and Ivens, 1886, I, pp. 225–227.
[66] Schinz, 1891, p. 346.   [67] Santos, 1898, pp. 500–501.
[68] *Le Philafricain*, I, 7, p. 27.   [69] Loeb, 1962, p. 143.
[70] Duparquet, 1880, p. 417.   [71] Loeb, 1962, p. 186.
[72] Gibson, 1905, p. 151; Pélissier, 1975, I, p. 545; AHA, Av–31–8–2, Chefe Humbe Relatório 12/7/1904.   [73] Stals, 1968. pp. 305–306; Portugal, 1903, part e.

Angola.[74] However, local southerners were also involved in the caravan system, especially the Ovambo.[75]

Traders from the colonial nucleus competed with African caravans for control over the mobile trade of the interior. In the period up to the 1880s, Portuguese traders formed their own caravans with employees or slaves, but they were not very successful in their attempts at taking over trade from the Mbali.[76] However, the introduction of ox-wagons from the 1880s gave more of an edge to the colonial traders. Wagons were well suited to the role of mobile shops, and owing to the general shortage of head-porters during the rubber boom, wagons were able to take over most of the mobile trade of the southern interior.[77] But the advent of lorries and trains from the 1910s spelled the end of the era of the peripatetic traders, who were increasingly replaced by a network of fixed stores.[78]

Wandering colonial traders were known to the Portuguese as *funantes*, the equivalent of the *smouses* of southern and central Africa. Often part-time or seasonal traders, they included many of the misfits and victims of colonial society, criminals, insolvent debtors, and adventurers of all kinds. The authorities were always complaining that the *funantes* indulged in slave trading, gun running, smuggling and other illegal activities, and that they were sources of disorder and even military expeditions.[79] But the *funantes* were irreplaceable in the early period, for their low overheads were essential for the profitability of trade in the interior. The *funantes* were also encouraged and protected by African chiefs, who found them an invaluable source of firearms and other goods which had been banned by the colonial authorities.[80]

Trade in the interior was to a great extent conducted on credit. African chiefs were deeply indebted to their suppliers, and repayment could be deferred over a period of many years.[81] The *funantes* were also advanced trade goods on credit by the coastal merchants, who in turn were sometimes indebted to Lisbon capitalists.[82] The most vulnerable agents in this chain of credit were the *funantes*, who were often unable to recoup their debts from African chiefs, while being subjected to harsh pressures on the part of the coastal merchants.[83] This difficult position undoubtedly accounts for the various unscrupulous methods used at times by the

[74] Childs, 1969, chapter 12.
[75] Loeb, 1962, p. 144; Andersson, 1856, pp. 171–175.
[76] McKiernan, 1954, pp. 107–108.
[77] Postma, 1897, p. 243.   [78] Mendes, 1958, pp. 34–36.
[79] Almeida, 1912, pp. 529–534; Braz, 1918, p. 170.
[80] Braz, 1918, p. 170; Angebauer, 1927, pp. 146–147 and passim.
[81] Duparquet, 1880, p. 417.
[82] Duparquet, 1881, p. 569; FO, *AS*, 2555, 1899.
[83] Galvão, 1944, p. 500.

funantes in order to escape from the vicious circle of debt peonage and the dangers of life in the bush.

Competition between traders attached to different ports was also acute, and the hinterland of Moçâmedes fluctuated accordingly. The Huíla highlands came within the more-or-less permanent sphere of influence of Moçâmedes after the foundation of this latter settlement in 1840, although the northern fringes of the area maintained commercial contacts with Benguela.[84] Traders from Moçâmedes or their agents had also penetrated the Ovambo and Okavango regions by 1850[85] and had reached Barotseland by 1875.[86] During the rubber boom, traders from the Huíla highlands reached the Lunda empire in the north-east and went through Barotseland and into the Kafue basin beyond.[87] Nevertheless, Moçâmedes rarely or never held commercial preponderance beyond the Huíla highlands, where agents of the Benguela–Lobito and Swakopmund–Walvis Bay complexes were always able to control much of the trade.[88]

The trade route to Moçâmedes was beset by two major problems: lack of water in the Namib desert and the steep face of the escarpment. This latter physical barrier presented formidable communication problems everywhere in south-western Africa, but nowhere was it so steep and unsurmountable as in the immediate hinterland of Moçâmedes.[89] As for the Namib desert, it was virtually impossible to cross in years of severe drought with porters or ox-wagons, as the water tanks in the middle ran dry.[90] The excellent natural port of Moçâmedes was thus largely wasted for trading purposes until the widening and extension of the railway in the 1960s, for the light railway built from 1905 was of little use in overcoming the obstacle of the escarpment.[91] In addition to transport problems, the consolidation of colonial frontiers had an adverse effect on the trade of Moçâmedes as northern South West Africa and western Northern Rhodesia were progressively closed to Portuguese traders.[92]

The most difficult aspect of trade in the interior concerns the vexed question of the nature and evolution of the terms of trade. There is sufficient statistical evidence to make tentative statements as to the terms of trade on the coast, but the occasional and dispersed figures for prices in the interior yield no consistent overall picture. On the coast, it would appear that the comparative evolution of prices of exported tropical

[84] Pinto, 1881, I, p. 53.   [85] Brochado, 1855.
[86] Holub, 1881, II, pp. 151–152.
[87] Pélissier, 1975, I, p. 359, for Lunda; NAZ, KTJ/1/1/1, Van Gielgud to Administrator N.E. Rhodesia 21/11/1900; NAZ, BS2/159, Bricker to Harding 27/2/1900.
[88] *J de M*, 20/3/1885.   [89] Urquhart, 1963, passim.
[90] Möller, 1974, pp. 20–21, 29–30.   [91] Galvão, 1930, pp. 100–104.
[92] Stals, 1968, pp. 316, 320; NAZ, KDE/8/1/1, Annual Report Barotse District 1906–1907.

commodities and imported manufactured goods was favourable to the former during most of the period under consideration.[93] But it would seem that this favourable edge of tropical goods was not necessarily carried over into the interior.

A variety of different factors worked against the African producer, with a tendency to get worse towards the end of the nineteenth century. Portuguese tariffs were always protectionist, but this became much more marked after the tariff reform of 1892, so that the prices of imported goods went up accordingly.[94] Furthermore, both firearms and alcohol were increasingly subjected to a whole range of additional taxes and controls towards the end of the nineteenth century.[95] Controls were widely avoided because of the endemic corruption within the Portuguese bureaucracy, but this also put up the final price paid by the consumer.[96] The direct producer within African societies was also subjected to a growing level of internal taxation or even outright seizures on the part of chiefs, who in many cases formed yet another set of middlemen between the producer and the market.[97] Finally, the high cost of transport in the age of porters and wagons worked against the producers in the interior, who were paid correspondingly less for their produce and had to pay more for their purchases.

The difference between the price paid for certain staple commodities in the interior and the price they fetched on the coast may be illustrated by a few examples, in the absence of continuous series of statistics. In 1896, an ox could be bought in the Huíla highlands for between £1 and £1.50 and sold on the coast for about £3.25.[98] In 1900, a pound of rubber fetched about 3p in eastern Angola and 15p on the coast.[99] In 1894, a slave would cost between £1.50 and £2.50 in the interior and between £8 and £12 on the coast.[100] The greatest profits seem to have been made between the interior and the coast, for in 1900 again, a pound of Angola rubber would fetch a maximum of only $17\frac{1}{2}$p on the London market.[101] This in turn explains the cut-throat competition for this very risky and often dangerous stage in the process of exchange.

The relations of production which underlay these economic activities in peasant societies were essentially of a lineage type.[102] Land and other

[93] Munro, 1976, pp. 45–46, 72, 144.   [94] Couceiro, 1910, pp. 364–365.
[95] Couceiro, 1910, pp. 80–83, 247–252; Coutinho, 1910.
[96] AHA, Av–41–90–5, GM to GG 7/10/1896.
[97] Clarence-Smith and Moorsom, 1975 and 1977.
[98] Santos, 1898, p. 450; *Estatística Commercial*, 1909, p. xv.
[99] NAZ, BS2/160, Harding Report 27/3/1900.
[100] Nascimento, 1898, p. 60.
[101] NAZ, BS2/160, Harding Report 4/7/1900.
[102] More precisely, primitive communist mode, complex redistribution variant –
see Hindess and Hirst, 1975, chapter 1.

productive resources were usually held in common and distributed for usufruct to homestead heads, or to specific individuals. Consumption and coordination of the labour process were limited in most cases to the homestead, although there was some cooperation between homesteads for a number of specific tasks such as hunting and raiding. Homesteads were almost entirely self-sufficient, and production for the market was never a predominant activity.

Within the homestead, division of labour was based primarily on sex but also on age. Women did the routine agricultural tasks, fishing and collecting for food. Men cleared the land, hunted, herded, raided and collected for the market. Specialization of labour on the basis of function was very limited, for all were required to perform the basic homestead tasks. Chiefs, smiths and witch-doctors were the most specialized functions, demanding a ritual sanction. Nor was there a clearly marked serf or slave stratum, for domestic slaves were often absorbed into the lineages which owned them. This was facilitated by the fact that only women and child slaves were usually retained, and these were easily assimilated in a polygynous society. Relations between homesteads were regulated by the distribution of three types of resources: women by marriage, cattle by inheritance and land by the decision of chiefs.[103]

Although these relations of production remained broadly predominant throughout the period under consideration, they were progressively eroded and modified by the effects of increasing articulation with the expanding capitalist mode of production. In an initial mercantile phase, capitalists were interested in the extraction of commodities from African tributary societies. This is true even if one considers slaves, in spite of the inherently ambiguous status of slaves as both commodities and labour power. In a second phase, which only became marked in the twentieth century, capitalists became increasingly interested in the extraction of labour power from African societies, in the form of migrant labour.[104]

During the mercantile phase of capitalist expansion, African tributary societies began to apportion more labour to petty commodity production for the market and became more dependent on imported manufactured goods, especially firearms. But the increased labour expended on petty commodity production does not seem to have involved any decrease in subsistence activities. This was probably because leisure time was being converted into labour time and because imports such as firearms increased the productivity of labour.[105] Domestic slaves obtained by more efficient raiding were also used to expand subsistence production.[106]

[103] Estermann, 1956–1961 and 1964; Loeb, 1962.
[104] Wolpe, 1974, for a general discussion of these points.
[105] Moorsom, 1973, section 3.   [106] Urquhart, 1963, p. 88.

69

From the 1910s, petty commodity production came under severe strains. Raiding was prevented by colonial authorities and hunting was reduced to a minor activity as a result of the extermination of game and the increasingly enforced colonial laws on hunting and firearms. Collecting also subsided after the collapse of the rubber boom. Petty commodity production thus came to centre almost exclusively on cattle raising, and it seems clear that the labour time expended in production for the market must have decreased significantly.[107]

The decline in petty commodity production was accompanied by the steady development of migrant labour, which corresponded to the growing demand for such labour in the colonial nuclei of Angola and South West Africa. The construction of the Benguela and Moçâmedes railways in the 1900s resulted in the first large-scale need for migrant labour in southern Angola,[108] and this was followed by the abolition of quasi-slavery after 1910 and the growth of contract labour in plantations and fisheries.[109]

In South West Africa, the Germans had been struggling with a growing labour crisis since the outbreak of the Herero revolt in 1904. The war of extermination waged against the Herero and Nama drastically reduced the local supply of labour, while increasing the acreage given over to white farmers. The almost simultaneous opening up of the Otavi copper mines in 1906 and the Lüderitz diamond fields in 1908 created an acute shortfall of labour, which was compounded by the accelerated programme of railway and harbour construction. The northern marches of the colony and adjoining regions of Angola thus came to be seen as a vital reservoir of labour by the Germans and by their South African successors.[110]

Migrant labour from the interior of southern Angola began on a small scale in the 1880s and grew slowly in subsequent years.[111] There was a sudden expansion in the late 1900s, as thousands of men went to work on the railways and mines of Angola and South West Africa.[112] From then on, the rate of labour migration fluctuated but remained at a level which made it of great economic importance to African tributary societies.[113] However, migrant labour did not disrupt the basic production relations outlined above, as labourers generally left for short periods during the slack season in the agricultural cycle, a time which had earlier been devoted to hunting, raiding, collecting or trading.[114]

But it would be mistaken to see migrant labour as a simple substitute for petty commodity production. Firearms ceased to be a necessary import

[107] Galvão, 1930, pp. 262–264; Statham, 1922, pp. 152–153; Rates, 1929, pp. 96–97.
[108] *P em A*, 149, May 1906, p. 225.   [109] See chapter 3, pp. 32–34.
[110] Clarence-Smith and Moorsom, 1975, pp. 377–378.
[111] Estermann, 1956–1961, I, p. 146.
[112] Clarence-Smith and Moorsom, 1975, p. 377.
[113] Galvão, 1930, pp. 237–243.   [114] Nitsche, 1913, pp. 134–136.

with the decline of hunting and raiding and the loss of political indepen-dence. African societies reverted to a much greater degree of economic self-sufficiency. The flow of migrant labour thus had to be underpinned by a considerable amount of direct or indirect coercion, in the absence of attractive wages and working conditions. Taxation everywhere and forced labour in Angola became the basic causes for the phenomenon of migrant labour from the late 1910s, and from an earlier date in certain areas. Migrant labour can be seen as an alternative to petty commodity pro-duction only during a brief transitional period in the 1900s and early 1910s. Similarly, land shortage and the deterioration of subsistence production began to affect migrant labour only in the 1930s and became of central importance in some areas only in the 1950s.[115]

It has been argued here that increased articulation with the capitalist mode of production modified but did not alter the basic relations of production within the peasant economy. Neither private ownership of the means of production nor the development of a class of labourers per-manently separated from the means of production occurred. Nevertheless, the modifications which resulted from increased articulation with the capitalist mode of production did have significant repercussions in the social and political spheres. These were heightened and distorted by the imposition of colonial rule and the implantation of christian missionaries. The following chapter is thus devoted to these various changes in African tributary societies.

[115] Moorsom, 1977.

6

Peasant societies

In order to grasp the changes which affected peasant societies in southern Angola, it is necessary to begin by presenting a more complete picture of what is meant by lineage social formations. In the previous chapter, emphasis was placed on communal ownership of the means of production, the relative self-sufficiency of the homesteads, and the sexual division of labour. To these must be added the social, political and ideological structures, which are essential for the existence and reproduction of the lineage mode of production as a whole. However, it must be stressed that the empirical material presented below is drawn from ethnographic studies on the farmer–herders of southern Angola, who make up the great bulk of the peasantry of the region.[1] The hunter–gatherers have been left out altogether, as being of negligible historical importance, and the predominantly farming societies of south-eastern Angola differ in many important details from the farmer–herders. Some of these differences are considered in the latter part of this chapter.[2]

Everyone in the farmer–herder societies belonged to two fundamental kinship groupings, tribes and clans, defined on the basis of endogamy and exogamy respectively. Endogamous tribes owned all the land in common, the prohibition on marriages outside the tribe serving to avoid any conflicts over land allocation. A hierarchy of chief and headmen existed for the purpose of arbitrating in the allocation of lands, but chief and headmen could not exclude families from sufficient land for their domestic needs. Chief and headmen did not own the land, in the strict marxist sense of ownership,[3] but rather exercised organizational and arbitrating functions with regard to communally owned land.

Each tribe was divided into a number of exogamous clans, which served

---

[1] The empirical material in the following paragraphs is based on: Estermann 1956–1961, 1964, 1976; Loeb, 1962.

[2] See pp. 88–96.

[3] Hindess and Hirst, 1975, pp. 233–242 and passim.

in particular to regulate the inheritance of cattle. Clans were matrilineal, but women moved to their husbands' homesteads on marriage. Sisters' sons, the most usual heirs in the case of the death of an old cattle owner, were thus widely spread through the tribal area. When an elder died, his cattle did not go to his sons, who lived with or near him, but instead to his numerous male matrilineal relatives in different areas. As a man could not marry a woman of the same clan as his own, there was no way in which cattle could remain in the homestead of an elder after death, although a man could give some cattle to his sons during his life-time. Long-term concentrations of cattle in a matrilineal descent group were also avoided by the very egalitarian manner in which cattle were distributed through inheritance. In a sense, one can say that cattle were owned collectively by the clan and were only entrusted to a man during his life-span.

In spite of these long-term structures of communal ownership and redistribution, very considerable inequalities existed in terms of access to the means of production as between elders and juniors. Elders not only accumulated large herds of cattle, but they also had more wives and could therefore farm a wider area. Marriage was often long delayed for young men, and even after marriage a young man might have to continue to live in his father's homestead until he had accumulated sufficient cattle to set up on his own. Nevertheless, it was impossible for this temporary inequality to become frozen into a hereditary class structure. No elder could pass on his advantages to a single heir, and all juniors could expect to become elders in their turn.

These relations of production were underpinned by various ideological and legal mechanisms. The worship of chiefly and commoner ancestors and the initiation rites for girls and boys reinforced kinship structures. At the same time, witchcraft accusations served to keep social inequalities within acceptable limits. Chiefs and headmen also acted as judges and law-enforcers with respect to executions for witchcraft or transgressions of marriage prohibitions and inheritance laws. However, there was no state in the strict sense of a specialized apparatus used by one class to maintain and reproduce its domination over another. Chiefs and headmen merely fulfilled certain necessary functions of organization and coordination. This involved considerable violence, including fairly frequent death sentences, but it was not the violence of one class exercised against another. It was rather the violence of the social formation exercised by its agents against deviant or perceived to be deviant individuals, who threatened the reproduction of the social formation as a whole.[4]

Lineage societies in southern Angola responded to the intensified

[4] Hindess and Hirst, 1975, p. 41 and passim.

73

pressures of capitalism in the period before the consolidation of colonial rule in a number of different ways. Variations were due both to certain minor differences in the internal structures of peasant societies and to the precise nature and timing of the pressures to which they were subjected. From the multiplicity of responses, four have been singled out for analysis as having been the most significant in terms of the number of people affected and the structural modifications involved. Feudal tendencies in the flood plains, social banditry in the highlands, mission theocracies among the Ngangela and the development of an independent peasantry in south-eastern Angola are therefore examined in turn. None of these responses were revolutionary in nature, in that they did not arise from fundamental internal structural crises within these societies and they did not result in the permanent transformation of the relations of production. They were rather crises caused by external factors, all related in some way to the expansion of triumphant nineteenth-century European capitalism.

However, the extension and consolidation of colonial rule from the 1900s onwards largely erased the differences between the reactions of specific peasant societies. Feudal nobles, social bandits, mission theocrats and independent peasants were all swept away to make room for a relatively uniform subject peasantry, which was obliged to provide commodities or labour power on the terms dictated by colonial officials. Nevertheless, the varying autonomous responses of an earlier period of articulation with capitalism left traces and did not disappear immediately or altogether. There are still differences between the social formations of southern Angola, the origins of which may be traced to the crucial formative decades of the late nineteenth and early twentieth centuries.

The partial emergence of feudal relations of production in the flood plains from the 1860s formed the first major response to articulation with capitalism, and in order to clarify the argument it is necessary to begin by a brief definition of the sense in which feudalism is being used here. In a feudal mode of production, the means of production are owned by the dominant class, and the dominated class is only allowed access to the means of production if it pays rent or tribute. These payments are used to maintain a state apparatus which enforces the unequal relations between the classes. Other features which are often associated with feudalism, such as the existence of a group of wealthy idlers or the unfree personal status of the dominated individuals, may often be found in a feudal social formation but are not structurally necessary for its existence.[5]

The system which evolved in the flood plains was only feudal to a certain degree. A dominant class extracted tribute by force from the majority of the population and used the tribute to maintain and equip a

[5] Hindess and Hirst, 1975, chapter 5; Hindess and Hirst, 1977, pp. 68–72.

standing army, which in turn ensured the extraction of tribute. The dominant class also engaged in a fair amount of conspicuous consumption. But the permanent separation of the direct producers from the means of production was not achieved and does not even seem to have been attempted. In other words, the exaction of tribute by force was never converted into the seizure of land and its holding according to a régime of private property. The most fundamental characteristic of a feudal mode of production was thus lacking, and one cannot consider that there was any real transition from lineage to feudal relations of production. It is possible that such a transition might have occurred in time, had not the colonial state intervened, but it is equally valid to speculate that these developments would only have proved to be a temporary aberration.

To understand why the societies of the flood plains reacted in this particular way, it is necessary to consider first the ecological conditions which led to an unusual degree of concentration of power in the hands of the chiefs. The density of population made central coordination easier and more efficient, and the complex patterns of flooding rendered land allocation more complicated than in the surrounding bush. Deforestation had to be carefully checked in the semi-arid environment and fruit trees needed especial protection. The decision as to when to begin planting was also unusually difficult in this area of slight and irregular rainfall and unreliable floods.[6]

The most important factor underlying the concentration of organizational powers in the hands of chiefs was probably the need to dig and maintain large reservoirs to stock the flood waters during the dry season.[7] The soil from these man-made lakes was piled up around the reservoirs and planted with fruit trees.[8] Large numbers of workers were required for this laborious task. In 1883, a missionary reported that about 300 men were toiling under the personal supervision of an Mbadya chief to dig a reservoir about forty feet deep.[9] In 1907, a Portuguese officer described two reservoirs as being roughly circular, twenty to thirty yards in diameter and so deep that cattle could swim in them.[10] Reservoirs were particularly vital in Ovamboland, where there was no permanent river, and it is interesting to note that the fullest development of chiefly powers occurred precisely in this part of the flood plains.

The concentration of commodities in the hands of chiefs may have been linked to the need to feed and recompense this labour force.

[6] Loeb, 1962, pp. 42–44 and 71; Lebzelter, 1934, passim.
[7] Urquhart, 1963, p. 40; McKiernan, 1954, p. 104.
[8] AGCSSp, 465–III, Duparquet 'Notes sur les différentes tribus des rives du Cunène'.
[9] AGCSSp, 478–B–II, Duparquet to TRP 25/7/1883.
[10] Castro, 1908, pp. 185–186.

75

Traditional rights to the seizure of young girls and cattle increased the milk, meat and grain at the chiefs' disposal.[11] Similarly, the chiefs received half the cattle and captives taken in raids, which had much the same effects.[12] The ground tusk of any elephant killed and most of the profits of trade and justice also accrued to chiefs.[13] But it is essential to stress that before the mid-nineteenth century, the concentration of goods in the hands of chiefs does not seem to have resulted in any significant measure of personal appropriation on the part of chiefs, who acted rather as central clearing houses in a complex pattern of social redistribution.[14]

The first steps in the transformation of chiefs into an exploiting class occurred with the importation of firearms and horses from the 1860s. Owing to their control over the trading process, chiefs were able to exercise a relatively efficient monopoly over supplies of horses and firearms. They then used these articles to arm personal bodyguards of young men, who came to be known as *lenga*.[15] This process took place in a period when firearms were undergoing a crucial technological revolution, which began in the 1860s and culminated in the 1880s. The new breech-loading repeating rifles, with their cartridges of copper and lead and smokeless powder, were a far cry from the trade muskets of an earlier generation.[16] Instead of the whole people being armed with cheap but useless muskets, there arose a situation in which a small group of skilled men controlled extremely efficient weapons.[17] Nor did horses become generally available as in the Americas, for even 'salted' horses died easily in the hot and humid flood plains.[18] Horses and rifles thus remained highly prized luxuries, which the chiefs kept for their trusted *lenga*.[19] Lastly, it should be recalled that horses and rifles were important producer goods, of great economic advantage in raiding and hunting.

But the formidable potential for exploitation represented by the *lenga* only began to be put into effect when a crisis arose with the exhaustion of ivory supplies through ruthless hunting. The chiefs were deep in debt to traders and they had become accustomed to consuming a certain number of imported luxuries, as had the *lenga*. Furthermore, sophisticated weapons were increasingly becoming necessary for protection against African and European threats.[20] In this situation, the chiefs turned to cattle and slaves as export commodities with which to replace ivory, but

11 Estermann, 1956–1961, I, pp. 141–142.
12 Estermann, 1956–1961, I, p. 144.   13 Nogueira, 1880, p. 267.
14 Nogueira, 1880, passim.   15 Hahn, 1867, pp. 292–293.
16 *Chamber's Encyclopaedia*, 1968, V, pp. 646–648.
17 AHU, 2R–15P, Ramalho, Relatório 20/6/1891.
18 Postma, 1897, p. 237; Möller, 1974, p. 32.
19 AHU, Companhia de Moçâmedes, 9, Chefe Humbe to GM 5/1/1896.
20 Duparquet, 1880, pp. 416–417, and 1881, p. 569.

people and cattle were essential productive resources which had to be taken from somebody. Increased raiding provided something of a solution to this problem, but internal taxation also had to be introduced.

The easiest way to secure large numbers of cattle and slaves was to intensify the scope and scale of traditional raiding activities, and the *lenga* enjoyed certain advantages in this respect. With their horses and rifles, they terrorized the weak and decentralized Ngangela and Wiko peoples, and protection payments could be exacted by the mere threat of raids.[21] The Portuguese could do little to prevent raids in the 1890s, owing to the severe financial crisis. The *lenga* were also able to cash in on the rubber boom by seizing rubber from caravans, and they occasionally obtained some ivory as well.[22] The proceeds of raids were shared between the *lenga* and the chiefs, some to be sold to traders, the rest to be retained in the form of cattle and slaves for the homesteads of chiefs and *lenga*.[23]

But raiding proved insufficient to satisfy the growing appetites of chiefs and *lenga*. In part, this was due to an unprecedented series of natural disasters – droughts, floods, locusts and cattle diseases – which swept through southern Angola from the 1890s to the 1910s and culminated in the terrible famine of 1915–1916.[24] Resistance to raids also became more effective, especially from the mid-1900s, when the Portuguese emerged from the throes of the financial crisis.[25] Lastly, the terms of trade became increasingly unfavourable as colonial governments clamped down on the sale of modern rifles to African peoples.[26]

Chiefs and *lenga* therefore fell back on the ever harsher taxation of their subjects, a process which was particularly marked in the largest tribe of the region, the Kwanyama of northern Ovamboland.[27] The *lenga* roamed the country at will, seizing cattle and young people of either sex to sell to traders or incorporate into their homesteads and that of the chiefs.[28] The chief of the Kwambi of central Ovamboland even forced the young men to go and work for the whites and bring back cattle to himself as tribute.[29] Accusations of witchcraft were also increasingly manipulated by chiefs in order to seize the property of the accused.[30] By 1907, a missionary observed that the Kwanyama had become divided into two

[21] AGCSSp, 476–B–V, Keiling to TRP 14/7/1914.
[22] AHU, 1R–21P, GB, Relatório 9/12/1901.
[23] Estermann, 1956–1961, I, pp. 141, 144.
[24] Clarence-Smith, 1974. [25] *P em A*, 148, April 1906, pp. 207–208.
[26] Couceiro, 1910, pp. 80–87, 247–252.
[27] Loeb, 1962, pp. 28–38; Estermann, 1956–1961, I, pp. 141–142.
[28] Möller, 1974, p. 113; AHU, Companhia de Moçâmedes, 9, Chefe Humbe to GM 5/1/1896; AHU, 1R–15P, Meisenholl to Chefe Humbe 29/11/1894, in GG to Minister 15/1/1895.
[29] Möller, 1974, p. 117. [30] Möller, 1974, pp. 126–127.

clearly distinguished camps, the oppressors and the oppressed, and that fighting between the two had become a common occurrence.[31]

The tensions within the societies of the flood plains were made worse by the fact that the *lenga* generally did not belong to the royal clan or leading commoner families. They were 'new men', who owed their position entirely to the discretion of the chiefs.[32] Some were sons of chiefs, excluded by matrilineal succession rules from inheriting the goods and positions of their fathers.[33] Others were ambitious young commoners of little or no standing.[34] Yet others were refugees from other tribes or even slaves, and these were the most resented by the population.[35] In many cases, the *lenga* usurped the functions of local headmen, and they retained the position of headman when they had become too old for raiding and tax collecting.[36]

With the consolidation of the powers of chiefs and *lenga* came an increasingly luxurious standard of living. As early as the 1870s, the chief of the Kwambi had mercilessly seized the cattle of his subjects in order to have a mediaeval castle built for himself, and he had filled it with a curious assortment of imported goods, from fiddles to wagons.[37] In the late 1890s, the Nkhumbi chief of Mulondo was attempting to live like a European gentleman, taking lessons on the smallest matters of etiquette from an ex-slave maid who had worked for the Portuguese.[38] But it was in the Kwanyama chieftaincy in the last years of its independence that these tendencies became most striking. In the 1910s, chief and *lenga* were immaculately dressed in suits and ties; they were great consumers of the best champagne, cognac and port, and were entertained by displays of fireworks. In addition, they possessed beautiful horses and the most expensive modern rifles.[39] All around, their people were starving and dying in one of the worst famines ever known.[40] This society had already come a long way from primitive communism.

At the other end of the social spectrum from the *lenga*, there emerged a new pauperized stratum of men with few or no cattle.[41] However, these men were not permanently divorced from the means of production. They still had unimpeded access to agricultural and grazing lands, and they could still recoup their losses in cattle. Indeed, they stood to gain by inheriting cattle at the death of a prominent *lenga* of their clan. There was

[31] *BG*, XXIV, 252, p. 455.
[32] Loeb, 1962, pp. 29–32.
[33] Loeb, 1962, pp. 29–32.
[34] Loeb, 1962, pp. 29–32.
[35] AGCSSp, 478–B–III, Duparquet to ? 26/3/1885; Angebauer, 1927, p. 188 and note.
[36] Vidal, 1912, p. 163.
[37] McKiernan, 1954, pp. 103–104; Duparquet, 1881, pp. 485–486.
[38] Rogado, 1957, pp. 80–91.
[39] Vidal, 1912, pp. 167–169; Keiling, 1934, pp. 171, 175.
[40] Clarence-Smith, 1974.
[41] Angebauer, 1927, pp. 112–113.

thus no structural and permanent creation of a class without direct access to the means of production, but merely the arbitrary and temporary impoverishment of unfortunate individuals. The loss of cattle was sufficient to create severe social tensions but not true social classes. The resistance of the commoners to the *lenga* was thus not so much a class struggle as a struggle to prevent the emergence of classes.

Apart from outbursts of violent resistance to the tax-raising activities of the *lenga*,[42] there were more organized forms of collective action on the part of the oppressed. In the 1870s, the Mbalantu of western Ovamboland killed their chief, abolished the institution of chieftaincy and absolutely prohibited the entry of white traders in their lands.[43] In 1885, a particularly tyrannical and rapacious chief of the Kwanyama was murdered during a popular insurrection, and the resident white traders were violently expelled.[44] However, in this latter case, the check to class formation was only very temporary, for within a few years the whole process began again.[45] There are also references to the growth of banditry in the Nkhumbi lands, but it is not clear whether this was a response to internal class formation or to Portuguese activities in and around the Humbe fort from the 1880s.[46]

As the power of chiefs and *lenga* became ever greater, collective resistance became less feasible and was replaced by large-scale emigration. Increasing numbers of families escaped with their cattle to settle in other tribal areas or to seek the protection of the whites.[47] In early 1896, there were an estimated 2,000 Kwanyama settled around the fort at Humbe, who had come to seek protection from the demands of the *lenga*. However, the places of these refugees in Kwanyama territory had been taken by other refugees from the Kwambi and Ndonga peoples to the south.[48] Flight to mission stations provided another alternative, although the missionaries could not take too many refugees for fear of the wrath of the *lenga*.[49] By the late 1900s, the effects of famine were added to those of social oppression, and emigration from the Kwanyama area was considerable.[50] In 1906, Kwangali families from the Okavango were to be found as far away as Barotseland.[51]

But although many men took the drastic step of permanent exile with

[42] *BG*, XXIV, 252, p. 455.   [43] McKiernan, 1954, p. 107.
[44] AGCSSp, 478–B–III, Duparquet to ? 26/3/1885 and Duparquet to TRP 26/8/1885.
[45] Loeb, 1962, pp. 29–32.
[46] AHA, Av–32–1–10, Veiga, Relatório 13/6/1905.
[47] Möller, 1974, pp. 95, 113–114, 117.
[48] AHU, Companhia de Moçâmedes, 9, Chefe Humbe to GM 5/1/1896.
[49] *BG*, XXIV, 252, pp. 455–456.
[50] AHA, Av–31–9–4, Moraes, Relatório 27/2/1909.
[51] Livingstone Museum MSS Collection, M/73/11, Rapport Lukona, 1906.

their whole families, a more common response from the 1900s onwards was for pauperized men to engage in migrant labour, especially to the mines of South West Africa.[52] The chiefs did not oppose this trend, but on the contrary welcomed it as an additional source of revenue and a way of retaining some social cohesion. Workers were only allowed to leave for short periods of about six months, at times when the agricultural cycle required least labour. They left in structured groups under leaders appointed by the chiefs, and refused to be split up in their places of work.[53] On return, they had to make a large 'present' to the chiefs for the privilege of having been allowed to leave.[54] At times, the migrant labourers would also be attacked and despoiled by the chief of another tribe as they returned home.[55] In general terms, migrant labour provided an important stabilizing factor for societies threatened with internal disruption and a falling cattle population.[56] It is even possible to speculate that the growth of migrant labour to South West Africa prevented a decisive struggle from occurring between the *lenga* and the people.

There were also internal efforts to lessen social tensions made by various chiefs, and the most notable of these was Mandume, who became chief of the Kwanyama in 1911. He was to have been killed at birth in order to avert a potential succession crisis, but he had narrowly escaped and had lived the life of a hunted exile as a child. He bore a large scar on his face, received during those difficult early years, and he never married.[57] His accession to the throne was strongly contested, and he seems to have been unpopular with the *lenga*.[58] This background may in part account for the changes which he attempted to make in the few years granted to him by the colonial powers.

Mandume attempted to reduce the growing conflicts in the Kwanyama chieftaincy by centralizing power in his own hands and imposing a more ordered system of taxation. He curbed the growing independence of the *lenga* and tried to turn their arbitrary exactions into a regular and generally imposed tax. He also chose his *lenga* mainly from outside the tribe, to ensure that their loyalty was to him alone. Judicial proceedings were further centralized at his court and it was decreed that there would be no more executions as a result of witchcraft accusations. Mandume

52 Clarence-Smith and Moorsom, 1977, pp. 105–106.
53 Schlettwein, 1907, p. 255; Nitsche, 1913, pp. 134–136; Deutschland, 1910, p. 128, and 1911, p. 109.
54 Schlettwein, 1907, p. 255; Estermann, 1956–1961, I, p. 146.
55 Nitsche, 1913, p. 136; AHA, Av–31–11–2, Capitão–Mor Cuamato to GH 6/5/1914.
56 AHU, Companhia de Moçâmedes, 9, Chefe Humbe to GM 5/1/1896 for social dislocations and falling cattle population.
57 Loeb, 1962, pp. 33–38; Keiling, 1934, p. 174; Angebauer, 1927, p. 198.
58 Angebauer, 1927, pp. 151–152; Braz, 1918, pp. 12–13.

enforced these measures with a degree of brutality which astonished even his hardened countrymen, and he would wander about the country in rags, disguised as a pauper, to see that his orders were being obeyed and that his subjects were not being victimized. He also broke many of the taboos which limited the actions of chiefs, such as the prohibitions on chiefs leaving the tribal area or leading armies in person.[59]

Mandume was equally intransigent in his rejection of white encroachments. Missionaries were strictly confined to the districts in which their stations were located, and all christian girls were forced to go through initiation rites, although these were forbidden by missionaries.[60] With the catholics, relations deteriorated to the point of violent expulsion. Mandume accused the catholics of collaborating with the Portuguese army, and in 1912 their station was razed to the ground and burned. The lives of the missionaries were spared, but they were not allowed to return to Kwanyama territory.[61] Nor would Mandume envisage any kind of arrangement with the Portuguese, whereby they would have a fort and a resident in his lands.[62] And he was extremely angry with the Germans for imposing a total ban on traders entering his lands.[63]

But nothing could stop the inexorable advance of colonial forces, especially after the introduction of machine-guns, although the Portuguese found the peoples of the flood plains to be their toughest opponents in Angola. Between 1885 and 1898, the Portuguese fought several long and inconclusive campaigns to secure their control over the strategic fort at Humbe on the west bank of the Cunene, and the conquest of the whole Nkhumbi area was not completed until 1905. Between 1906 and 1909, all the Ovambo and Okavango peoples in Angola, with the important exception of the Kwanyama, were also conquered, but it was not till 1915 that Lisbon sent a really large metropolitan army to effect the final submission of the Kwanyama.[64] As for the Germans, they occupied the south bank of the Okavango during the 1900s, and imposed strong indirect pressures on the Ovambo in their sphere of influence.[65] But it was left to a South African expedition in 1917 to complete the conquest of Ovamboland and kill Mandume.[66]

After the final conquest of the flood plains, the momentum of class formation was broken but its effects did not disappear altogether. The

---

[59] Loeb, 1962, pp. 33–38; Lehmann, 1954–1955, pp. 288–291; Angebauer, 1927, pp. 185–196; Lima, 1977, pp. 75–81.
[60] Driessler, 1932, pp. 251–252, 256.
[61] AGCSSp, 476–B–V, Keiling to TRP 4/2/1913.
[62] Braz, 1918, pp. 12–13.   [63] Lehmann, 1954–1955, p. 289.
[64] Pélissier, 1975, I, pp. 582–708.
[65] Leutwein, 1907, pp. 188–190; Lehmann, 1954–1955, pp. 283–284 and passim.
[66] Gorges and de Jager, 1917.

chiefs and *lenga* could no longer raid and exact tribute, but they retained considerable powers and advantages as officials in the colonial system.[67] However, their position was increasingly threatened by the rise of a new stratum of educated youths, the so-called 'police-boys', who used their functions as interpreters and underlings of white officials to usurp many of the powers of the *lenga*.[68] But the *lenga* also managed to retain much of their wealth, especially through the control of their domestic slaves. Slaves and their descendants do not seem to have been completely absorbed into the kinship system, but rather to have continued to form a hereditary group of 'servants', attached to the families of their masters.[69] In the late 1930s, the contrast was still strong between the headmen, with their large herds, fine kraals and numerous dependants, and the poor monogamous commoners, who lived in 'poor, miserable, tumble-down kraals'. Indeed, many of these latter were never able to get married at all, and lived as dependants of the headmen.[70] However, a great deal more research is needed on the evolution of class formation after colonial conquest.

Social banditry in the Huíla highlands formed the second major peasant response to capitalist penetration. As Hobsbawm has shown, social banditry is a reaction to non-revolutionary crises in peasant societies. Bandits are supported and considered heroes by the population, and are thus not common robbers, but they are conservatives rather than revolutionaries. Their programme is the 'defence or restoration of the traditional order of things'. At times, one may get the 'noble robber' kind of bandit, who robs from the rich to give to the poor, but this would seem to be more a figure of legend than a frequent historical occurrence. More often, bandits are 'avengers', who strike down the enemies of the people. As such, bandits are often to be found in situations where a foreign conqueror dominates the area.[71]

In the Huíla highlands, social banditry developed with the arrival of white settlers, in the period preceding the consolidation of the authority of the colonial state. The first wave of land spoliation and resulting banditry occurred in the 1860s, when cotton cultivation was introduced in the foothills below the escarpment.[72] But the problem became much more acute with the settling of the Boers and Madeirans in the highlands proper

[67] Loeb, 1962, p. 37.
[68] Witwatersrand University Archives, Damaraland Diocesan Records, AB 851, Q.P. 25/7/1935.
[69] Loeb, 1962, pp. 124–126.
[70] Witwatersrand University Archives, Damaraland Diocesan Records, AB 851, article in *South African Outlook* 1/11/1938.
[71] Hobsbawm, 1969, pp. 13–14, 21, 34–60, 88–89.
[72] Sousa, 1887, pp. 403–404.

after 1881. By 1900, there were 3,000 whites in the Huíla highlands, according to the somewhat inflated official estimates.[73] Rather more reliable figures for 1910 put the total at just over 3,000.[74]

However, the arrival of the settlers was accompanied neither by the military occupation of the whole region, nor by the uncontested supremacy of the colonial state. It was not until the 1900s that the Portuguese moved out of the northern half of the highlands to effectively conquer the surrounding areas.[75] At the same time, the settlers remained remarkably independent of the state apparatus and were largely a law unto themselves until the 1900s, especially the Boer trekkers.[76] Thus for two decades there existed a situation in many ways reminiscent of the Boer republics in South Africa before the mining revolution.

A bitter struggle over land was waged in the Huíla highlands during the early 1880s. In theory, the Portuguese government only granted 'vacant' lands to white settlers, but the governor general admitted in a confidential letter to his superiors that the distinction between vacant and occupied land was an impossible one to make, in view of the shifting cultivation and extensive pastoralism practised by the Nyaneka. Nor did the Portuguese have the staff to effectively survey the lands. The governor general therefore recommended that the rights of African peasants be ignored and that the state should concentrate on settling as many whites as possible in the area.[77] Local officials went even further, advocating the complete extermination of Africans and their replacement by white settlers.[78] The outcome was less drastic, but by 1885 the Boers and the Portuguese had succeeded in driving the Nyaneka off the best lands in the northern highlands. The exact proportion of land taken cannot be determined for lack of statistics, but the settlers took all the scarce alluvial lands along the little streams of the northern highlands, where the soils and rainfall were most propitious for agriculture.[79]

The struggle over land did not cease in 1885, but it became less acute. The failure of wheat cultivation and the very slow economic development of the region meant that the white population grew only gradually and that the demand for fresh lands was not great.[80] Many Nyaneka were able to resume access to their ancestral lands through squatting, share-cropping and labour tenancy agreements.[81] In the late 1880s, it was reported that

[73] Angola, 1901.   [74] Almeida, 1912, statistical tables.
[75] Details of campaigns in AHU, 4R, Pastas 2 and 5.
[76] Heese, 1976.
[77] AHA, Cod–A–16–2, GG to Minister 11/11/1882.
[78] AHA, Av–41–70–2, GM to GG 7/3/1884.
[79] Portugal, 1918, I, p. 376; Medeiros, 1976.
[80] See chapter 4, pp. 44–45.
[81] AGCSSp, 478–A–III, Antunes to TRP 28/5/1889; *C de M*, 28/11/1903, Campos letter; Diniz, 1914, pp. 82–83.

the Boers had practically driven all Africans off the Humpata plateau, but in 1902 settlements of whites and Africans were all mixed up in the same area.[82] However, there were many continuing disputes over land, and the Nyaneka never completely accepted the usurpation by the white settlers of the best lands in the area.[83] It is significant that, when the new republican authorities decided to begin to demarcate communal lands from freehold lands in the 1910s, the Huíla highlands formed one of the three areas in Angola where the problem was most acute.[84] However, it should also be recalled that the 1910s were a decade of renewed wheat cultivation in the highlands.[85]

Although Hobsbawm has stressed the importance of landlessness in the formation of bandit groups,[86] losses of cattle were probably equally important in southern Angola. The cattle which the Boers had brought from the Transvaal were not suited to local conditions and died in large numbers, so that the Boers turned to the Nyaneka to replenish their herds.[87] The campaigns for land in the early 1880s became campaigns for cattle as well. In a single small expedition in 1883, the Boers and Portuguese seized about 1,000 head of cattle.[88] In December of that same year, the authorities banned all private expeditions for the purpose of seizing cattle,[89] but the sources are full of complaints of Boer cattle raids during the 1880s and 1890s.[90] Cattle were also taken from the Nyaneka in more insidious ways, through the sharp trading practices of the *funantes*, who were usually backed by officials in any dispute.[91]

Slave raiding was on a much smaller scale than land and cattle spoliation. The labour needs of the settlers were small, as transport riding was not labour intensive and cattle could be tended by local Africans on a share-cropping basis.[92] Whenever there was a need for agricultural labour. *serviçaes* were obtained from the slave markets of central and northern Angola.[93] However, the Boers and Portuguese did engage in a little illicit slave raiding in the highlands.[94] The Nyaneka would also commend their children to settlers in times of famine, and these children were treated as slaves.[95] Some of the *serviçaes* held by settlers were thus of local origin.[96]

---

[82] AGCSSp, 477–A–I, Antunes to Bishop of Angola 1889; AHU, Documentos Importantes, 979, Carvalho, Relatório 20/11/1902.
[83] AHA, Av–31–5–7, GH to Diniz, 14/6/1913; Medeiros, 1976, pp. 423–424.
[84] Diniz, 1917, p. 6.   [85] Portugal, 1918, I, pp. 357–481.
[86] Hobsbawm, 1969, p. 25.   [87] Schinz, 1891, p. 346.
[88] AGCSSp, 478–B–II, Duparquet to TRP 27/4/1883.
[89] AHMH, 12, GM, Circular 1/12/1883.
[90] AHU, 1R–6P, GG to Minister 18/11/1886, for one example.
[91] Santos, 1898, pp. 500–501.   [92] Möller, 1974, pp. 17, 54.
[93] AHA, Cod–A–16–2, GG to Minister 11/11/1882.
[94] Almeida, 1912, p. 318.   [95] AHA, Av–41–71–2, GM to GG 4/2/1894.
[96] Staatsargief, Pretoria, A 779–I, Contractos, 1893.

In addition to these various forms of spoliation, the Nyaneka were forced to accept interference in the political and ideological spheres. Settlers, officials and missionaries frequently meddled in succession disputes, and they took over many judicial and arbitrating functions, keeping the fines and payments which in earlier times would have been redistributed by chiefs.[97] Missionaries posed an ideological challenge to Nyaneka society, and they were particularly unsympathetic to African culture and aspirations in this area.[98] There was a close identification between the mainly Portuguese personnel of the missions and the Madeiran settlers, so that Africans were faced with a settler church rather than a mission church, in spite of the strong protests of the mother house in Paris.[99] Missionaries were thus unable to mediate effectively between the settlers and the Nyaneka in such a way as to cushion the impact of settler violence.

The peasants who found these conditions intolerable and took to the hills were joined by representatives of two other social groups: soldiers and slaves. Deserters and ex-soldiers have always been important in social bandit movements, for they are rootless, discontented, skilled in warfare, but still very close to the peasant world.[100] In Angola, black recruits had every reason to desert. They were press-ganged, beaten, badly fed, paid months or years in arrears and not released at the end of their terms of service.[101] Indeed, in some cases, the soldiers were simply state slaves, bought from the slave dealers as the planters bought their *serviçaes*.[102] Another similar group which was represented in the bandit lairs consisted of unemployed mercenary auxiliaries, who were mainly Herero and Khoi refugees from South West Africa.[103] Escaped slaves from the plantations and fisheries also played a prominent role, much as serfs had done in earlier days in Russia.[104] All these various groups found a ready welcome in the bandit hide-outs.[105]

The daily life of bandits remains shadowy, although a certain amount can be pieced together from the sources. Easily defensible and well watered positions were chosen as base camps, especially in the rugged

---

[97] AHA, Av–41–71–2, Chefe Humpata to GM 15/3/1893, in GM to GG 22/3/1893; AHMH, 12, Chapman et al. to GM 9/12/1901 and Chefe Humpata to GM 26/12/1901.

[98] For example, *P em A*, 111, March 1903, p. 155.

[99] AGCSSp, 477–A–IV, Le Roy 'Administration de la mission du Cunène' 2/2/1907.

[100] Hobsbawm, 1969, pp. 27–2.   [101] Cid, 1894, pp. 14–15.

[102] AHM, 5P–23, GG to Chefe Novo Redondo 6/5/1884; NAZ, BS2/160, Harding, Report 27/3/1900.

[103] AHA, Av–41–70–6, GM to GG 6/4/1891.

[104] Hobsbawm, 1969, p. 27; see chapter 4, p. 37.

[105] AHA, Av–41–70–6, GM to GG 6/4/1891.

terrain and thick acacia forests of the southern highlands.[106] The bandits built rough fortresses, known as *cipaka*, on rocky outcrops, filling in gaps with boulders, palisades of sharp stakes or great thorn bushes.[107] In some cases, these *cipaka* could withstand sustained rifle fire and could only be taken with field artillery.[108] A certain amount of agriculture was carried out in remote and hidden valleys, and there always seem to have been a few women in these camps.[109] Wax and honey were also collected for sale to traders.[110] But the main source of bandit revenue came from cattle raids. Cattle were sold to unscrupulous *funantes*, who in turn provided the bandits with indispensable firearms and ammunition, as well as acting as spies for them.[111] In the 1920s, arms were also acquired with money earned by a spell of migrant labour in the mines of South West Africa.[112] The extent to which local peasants actively supported the bandits remains obscure, but there was undoubtedly widespread support for their cause.[113]

The leaders of the bandit groups were often drawn from the traditional hierarchy of Nyaneka chiefs, and it is possible to trace the career of one of these men. Mbundu was the nephew of one of the most powerful chiefs in the highlands and a potential heir to the chieftaincy. He was already active against the Portuguese in the foothills as early as 1875, and he was captured in 1882.[114] He was drafted into the colonial army in Luanda, but he deserted with his rifle and returned home in about 1887. The highlands resounded with the fame of his exploits in succeeding years, but he was taken by surprise by a force of white cavalry in 1901. All the men, women and children in his *cipaka* were slaughtered or burned alive, and Mbundu's head was exposed on a stake at the nearby settlement of Humpata.[115]

A similarly violent end was suffered by many of Mbundu's colleagues, and there seems to have been a gradual falling off of support for social bandits after the 1880s, as is illustrated by the career of another famous bandit leader. Mukakapira played a leading role in attempting to prevent the installation of a large colony of Madeirans in the Lubango valley in 1885. Expeditions were sent to dislodge him from his hide-out in the mountains overlooking Lubango, but Mukakapira repelled these expedi-

[106] AGCSSp, 477–A–V, Muraton to TRP 4/7/1893.
[107] *J de M*, 20/7/1885; personal observations Njau area 1973; Medeiros 1976, photographs opposite p. 108.
[108] *J de M*, 20/7/1885.
[109] *J de M*, 20/7/1885; AHU, 4R–2P, Chefe da coluna to GM 14/11/1901.
[110] AHA, Av–41–90–4, Mapa in annex to GM to GG 10/11/1887.
[111] AHU, 1R–22P, Chefe Gambos to GH 26/2/1905, in GG to Minister 25/4/1905.
[112] Galvão, 1930, p. 151.   [113] Paiva, 1938, I, pp. 258–259.
[114] AHU, 45P, GM to GG November 1875; *J de M* 20/6/1882; Wieder, 1892, p. 719.   ,
[115] *J de M*, 1/6/1887; Wieder, 1892, p. 719; AHU, 4R–2P, GM to Chefe d'Estado Maior 19/11/1901 and Chefe da Coluna to GM 14/11/1901.

tions and inflicted heavy losses on them. He was at the height of his fame in the late 1880s, but by 1892 pressures had become so strong that he was forced to abandon his *cipaka*. He then led a wandering life, increasingly rejected by the various chiefs into whose territory he came and losing men steadily. He was finally betrayed and captured in 1897, and shot by his escort in unexplained circumstances.[116]

The slackening of support for social bandits was due to a number of factors. In the first place, the bandits of southern Angola were 'avengers' rather than 'noble robbers',[117] and their role thus became less vital as the memories of the traumatic decade of the 1880s slowly faded. This trend was reinforced by the more severe restraint on Boer raiding implemented by the Portuguese, which nearly led to a full-scale Boer rebellion.[118] Secondly, settler resistance to the bandits became much more effective with the formation of a small squadron of irregular white cavalry in 1887 and the setting up of a force of metropolitan cavalry in Lubango in 1894.[119] But the most important reason was probably that the bandits began to prey as much on ordinary peasants as on the settlers, even seizing women and children to sell into slavery.[120] The bandits were crossing the invisible but crucial line which separates social banditry from common robbery.[121]

The difference between true social banditry and common robbery is best illustrated by the career of Oorlog, who was perhaps the most famous bandit of his time. Oorlog was the son of a Tswana, who had married the daughter of a Herero chief in central South West Africa. The whole family moved to southern Angola in the early 1880s, fleeing the disturbances caused by the Herero–Nama war.[122] In Angola, Oorlog set up a prosperous business as a mercenary on Portuguese expeditions into the interior, leading a motley collection of refugees from South West Africa and Angolan Herero, and gaining a great reputation as a fearless, cunning, skilful and ruthless fighter.[123] But when the Portuguese abandoned expeditions into the interior in the 1890s and set up the white cavalry unit in the highlands, Oorlog was out of a job, and he and his men took to a life of rapine.[124] The local Nyaneka were terrified of him, and did not dare to complain to the Portuguese authorities, as they thought he was still working for them.[125] He was pardoned by the Portuguese in 1905, as his services were required for renewed expansion into the interior, and two

[116] AHU, 1R–17P, Chefe Humpata to GM 13/2/1897, in GG to Minister 20/4/1897.
[117] Hobsbawm, 1969, pp. 34–60; AHU, 1R–2P, GG to Minister 27/3/1880.
[118] *P em A*, 45, September 1897, pp. 396–397.
[119] AHU, 2R–23P, GG to Minister 12/11/1897; *J de M*, 16/1/1894.
[120] AHA, Av–41–70–6, GM to GG 6/4/1891.
[121] Hobsbawm, 1969, p. 14.   [122] Van Warmelo, 1951, pp. 16–18.
[123] Nascimento, 1891, pp. 61–62, 106.   [124] Paiva, 1938, II, pp. 67, 81.
[125] AHU, 1R–22P, Chefe Gambos to GH 26/2/1905, in GG to Minister 25/4/1905.

years later he was appointed head of the newly formed native police, with a regular salary.[126] In this position, he played a key part in subjugating the strongholds of the social bandits between 1908 and 1910.[127] When his services were no longer needed, Oorlog took to a life of crime once again and was expelled by the Portuguese into the Kaokoveld of South West Africa, where the South African authorities recognized him as a Herero chief.[128]

Social banditry was brought under control by the colonial authorities in the 1900s. Military occupation was generalized throughout the region, and the Portuguese took the *cipaka* by storm between 1908 and 1910, with the help of Oorlog and field artillery.[129] Regular administration, taxation and forced labour replaced the arbitrary raiding by settlers.[130] After 1913, the Nyaneka became part of the labour pool designated for the plantations and fisheries of the coastal strip.[131] Nevertheless, the ideal guerilla territory of the southern highlands remained a magnet for malcontents of all kinds. An expedition was sent to deal with a renewed outbreak of social banditry in the late 1920s, but with no success.[132] In the 1940s, the Portuguese used aircraft for the first time in Angola to subdue the Herero of the foothills, accused of systematic cattle raiding.[133] And during the liberation struggle of the 1960s and 1970s, it was rumoured that the Nyaneka had taken to the hills again.[134]

Peasant responses in south-central and south-eastern Angola differed from the two case studies outlined above, partly because external pressures varied and partly because the internal social structures of African societies were not the same. Unfortunately, there exists no good ethno-grahic monograph for either the Ngangela or the Wiko peoples, but the following general points are fairly clear.[135] Cattle herding was not as important as in the highlands and flood plains, although cattle were everywhere present.[136] Population densities were lower, but individual villages were larger.[137] Tribal entities did exist, but chiefs had very few powers and most decisions were taken by village headmen.[138] Matrilinearity appears to have been the rule, although the Ngangela may have had patrilineal succession to political office.[139] Further than this, it is difficult to go.

126 Roçadas, 1919, pp. 149–151.   127 Almeida, 1912, pp. 151–152.
128 Galvão, 1930, p. 260; Van Warmelo, 1951, pp. 16–18.
129 Almeida, 1912, pp. 139–141, 529–534.   130 Almeida, 1912, p. 210.
131 Diniz, 1914, pp. 52–55.   132 Galvão, 1930, pp. 151–153.
133 Pélissier, 1975, I, pp. 744–754.
134 Personal communication of doubtful value, Sá da Bandeira 1973.
135 McCulloch, 1951 and Schachtzabel, 1923 are the best general works. Additional references given below.
136 *J de M*, 9/12/1881, Dufour letter 8/10/1880; Almeida, 1912, passim.
137 Delachaux, 1948, p. 63.
138 AGCSSp, 478–B–II, Duparquet to TRP 27/4/1883.
139 Keiling, 1934, p. 42; Sarmento, 1945, pp. 37–38.

The weak and scattered Ngangela of south-central Angola were subjected to intense Ovambo raiding during the late nineteenth century, and this led them to accept the formation of small mission theocracies, on lines reminiscent of the famous jesuit reductions of South America.[140] As in Paraguay, the catholic Holy Ghost Fathers, or spiritans, offered both military assistance against raiders and protection from colonial society. The missionaries were prepared to respect essential social and cultural structures, using indigenous languages and maintaining chiefly hierarchies, communal land tenure and redistribution of wealth. But the missionaries did impose certain new customs, in particular the practice of monogamy and stricter sexual morality. More important was the fact that the catholic priests took over many organizational and ideological functions. They also tended to be paternalist and authoritarian, with a strong belief in the natural inferiority of non-European peoples.[141] Mission theocracies thus represented the usurpation of certain functions in lineage societies by a group of outsiders in a time of stress, but there did not occur any radical modification in the basic relations of production.

The spiritans began by facing a strong challenge in the mid-1880s from one Ciwako, an ambitious Ngangela, who tried to resolve the problems facing his society in very different ways to the creation of theocracies. Ciwako was a village headman who was related to the chief of Katoko, the main Ngangela chieftaincy. Ciwako's strategy consisted in persuading the Portuguese to set up a fort by his village on the Okavango river, and then using the garrison and fort to gain protection from Ovambo raiding and to obtain cooperation in a scheme to usurp the chieftaincy of Katoko. It was further hoped that the Portuguese fort could be used to control and tax the trade in rubber, wax and ivory to Ciwako's profit, thus enabling him to build up an arsenal of modern weapons. This plan was initially successful, for the Portuguese were afraid of German expansion and set up a fort next to Ciwako's village in 1886.[142]

But these cunning schemes were unexpectedly ruined by the signing of the Luso–German frontier agreement in late 1886, for the sudden drop in international tension made the Okavango fort redundant.[143] In 1888, the garrison was withdrawn to the highlands and the Portuguese flag and formal political authority were entrusted to Ciwako's rivals, the local catholic missionaries. Ciwako therefore attacked the mission station and forced the missionaries to withdraw, alleging that they were responsible

---

[140] Caraman, 1975 for jesuits.
[141] Caraman, 1975; Kieran, 1966, for general view of spiritans.
[142] Paiva, 1938, I, pp. 53–112; AGCSSp, 475–A–VII, Lecomte 'Rapport pour la fondation d'une mission à l'Okavango' and 'Chez les Ganguellas'; *J de M*, 8/3/1889.
[143] AHU, 2R–11P, GG to Minister 11/1/1887 and 14/7/1887.

for the failure of the rains.[144] The spiritans campaigned in Lisbon for this affront to be avenged, and in 1889 an expedition was sent against the Ngangela. Ciwako was defeated, captured and exiled to the Cape Verde Islands.[145] However, he preferred to take his own life by jumping overboard loaded with chains, at least according to the official report.[146]

After the defeat of Ciwako, the Portuguese withdrew their forces once more, and the Ngangela fell back on the spiritans for protection.[147] The *lenga* from the flood plains spread ever greater terror and destruction during the 1890s and 1900s, and the mission stations represented the only hope of safety.[148] The Portuguese authorities allowed the missionaries to import modern rifles in order to arm a militia of christian youths, and regular shooting practices were held to improve the effectiveness of this home guard. Mission stations were converted into stockaded fortresses, in which Portuguese officials would sometimes take refuge.[149] The spiritans were also able to do something to repair the consequences of raids for local christians. The missionaries had close contacts with many of the chiefs of the flood plains, who were occasionally prepared to return captives and other booty at the missionaries' intercession.[150] Finally, the spiritans shielded Africans on and around mission stations from the sharp practices of traders and the labour demands of colonial officials.[151]

Two other old jesuit tactics were employed to win over the Ngangela: the systematic utilization of local language and a concentration on educating the heirs of chiefs. The spiritans did pioneering work in recording and writing down the Ngangela language and used it extensively in schools and in evangelization. Father Lecomte, the 'apostle of the Ngangela', came to have an obsession with Bantu languages and argued that they were extremely rich and subtle, capable of expressing such theological complexities as the trinity with remarkable economy and force.[152] Lecomte also turned away rapidly from traditional methods of evangelization, which were based on redeeming slave children, and concentrated instead on setting up schools for free children, especially the heirs of chiefs.[153] In time, these children became the first catechists and

---

144 *J de M*, 8/3/1889.
145 Paiva, 1938, I, pp. 113–158.
146 AHU, 1R–10P, GG to Minister 10/2/1890.
147 Nascimento, 1894, pp. 19–20.
148 AGCSSp, 476–B–II, Lecomte to ? 1/9/1899.
149 AGCSSp, 475–A–V, Lecomte 'Planalto do sul de Angola' 1896; *BG*, XX, 163, pp. 559–561, and 164, pp. 587–588.
150 For example, *BG*, XX, 163, pp. 558–559.
151 *Annales Apostoliques*, XVII, 6, August 1901, pp. 133–135.
152 AGCSSp, 476–B–II, Lecomte to TRP 30/1/1901; *Annales Apostoliques*, XVI, 7, September 1900, pp. 148–151.
153 AGCSSp, 475–A–VII, Lecomte to Duparquet, January 1887.

were very influential in spreading christianity.[154] In 1902, the chief of Katoko became a christian, and this was followed by a wave of conversions.[155] The spiritans then did their best to strengthen the position of the chief of Katoko among the Ngangela as a whole.[156]

But although the missionaries worked with the chiefly hierarchies, they also took many powers upon themselves. On mission stations, the resident priest was the main political as well as ideological functionary.[157] In 1910, an ecclesiastical visitor strongly criticized the assumption of wide administrative powers by missionaries, which had greatly antagonized local chiefs and headmen.[158] The extent to which this could go is illustrated by the fact that the local priest would inflict corporal punishment on christians found to have committed adultery.[159] Forced recruiting of children for schools was also reported, although not in the Ngangela region.[160] It appears that the missionaries were in effect considered as the chiefs of the areas around the mission stations.[161]

The mission stations were also centres of economic power. Subsidies were received from European charities, but from the 1890s the Portuguese government became the main source of funds.[162] In 1898, Lecomte even confessed that he had more money than he knew what to do with.[163] Mission stations were well equipped and produced a number of cash crops for the market, so that revenue from agricultural production increased fairly steadily.[164] But it must be stressed that missionaries did not benefit personally from this modest prosperity. Resources were used for the benefit of the christian community as a whole, and the living standards of missionaries were frugal and modest.[165] Nevertheless, the priests did have the important power of deciding exactly how funds would be spent.

The powers in the hands of missionaries were rendered less tolerable by the paternalist exclusion of Africans from positions of responsibility in the ecclesiastical hierarchy. Although the founder of the Ngangela missions had pleaded in the 1880s for a numerous African clergy,[166] the general mission attitude was that Africans were overgrown children, who required

[154] AGCSSp, 475–A–V, Lecomte 'Quelques idées sur l'aménagement et la marche d'une mission'.
[155] *BG*, XXII, 191, pp. 9, 14.
[156] Vidal, 1912, p. 453.
[157] *BG*, XVIII, 128, pp. 711–712.
[158] AGCSSp, 476–A–I, Cancella, Compte-Rendu 21/7/1910.
[159] AGCSSp, 476–B–V, Keiling to TRP 12/9/1913.
[160] AGCSSp, 477–A–X, Cancella, Rapports 1910.
[161] *BG*, XVIII, 128, pp. 711–712; AGCSSp, 476–B–V, Keiling to TRP 20/9/1911.
[162] AGCSSp, 475–B–I, II, and III, give yearly financial details.
[163] AGCSSp, 476–B–II, Lecomte to TRP 10/5/1898.
[164] AGCSSp, 476–A–III, Keiling, Rapport 1/3/1914; see also note 162.
[165] AGCSSp, 476–B–II, Lecomte to Pascal 31/1/1901.
[166] AGCSSp, 465–IV, Duparquet to TRP 21/6/1881.

constant supervision by whites.[167] The spiritans excited the ambitions of young men by fostering a limited 'revolution of youth', but young christians then found it very difficult to progress beyond the position of catechist.[168] In 1910, in the prefecture of Cimbebasia, which included the Ovimbundu and Ovambo missions, there were 23 white priests, 14 white lay brothers, 4 white sisters, 4 black sisters, 1 black lay brother and 118 black catechists.[169]

Mission theocracies were dependent on the support of the Portuguese government, and this was abruptly withdrawn as a result of the republican revolution of 1910. The violently anti-clerical republican authorities wanted to abolish religious missions completely, especially when they were staffed with foreigners, and replace them with Portuguese 'lay missions'.[170] In the Ngangela region, the new authorities accused the missionaries of having unlawfully usurped administrative powers belonging to the state and of encouraging Africans to disobey the new laws on taxation and forced labour.[171] Missionaries were arrested, tried and expelled, often on the basis of rather dubious evidence.[172] Subsidies from the government were also suspended.[173] Relations between church and state slowly improved, but it was not until the days of Salazar that amicable relations were restored.[174]

Local republican officials mounted an effective campaign to turn the Ngangela against the missionaries. Army officers stressed that the job of dealing with Ovambo raids now fell on them, and in 1915 the Ovambo menace was finally crushed. Many Ngangela catechists were recruited for these campaigns, gained new status as NCOs, and on their return became the greatest enemies of the missions.[175] The Ngangela were also encouraged to indulge in polygamy, divorce and drinking, and discouraged from being baptized or attending religious ceremonies.[176] In addition, the missionaries lost a great deal of prestige as a result of the persecutions to which they were subjected.[177] Between 1910 and 1914, the number of christians in the Katoko mission dropped from about 7,000 to about 5,000.[178] The prefect apostolic commented bitterly: 'Their fervour has

---

[167] AGCSSp, 475–A–V, Lecomte 'Extrait d'un discours' 3/6/1889; *BG*, XXVII, 318, p. 219; Kieran, 1969, pp. 345–347.
[168] *BG*, XX, 163, pp. 558–562.
[169] AGCSSp, 475–B–II and III, 476–A–II and VI, for yearly statistics.
[170] Marques, 1973, p. 392.
[171] AGCSSp, 476–B–V, Keiling to TRP 20/9/1911.
[172] See documents in Brásio, 1966–1971, V.
[173] AGCSSp, 476–B–V, Keiling to TRP 4/2/1913.
[174] Marques, 1973, p. 392.   [175] *BG*, XXVIII, 342, pp. 493–495.
[176] AGCSSp, 476–B–V, Keiling to TRP 12/9/1913.
[177] AGCSSp, 476–A–III, Keiling, Rapport 1/3/1914.
[178] AGCSSp, 476–A–III, Keiling, Rapport 1/3/1914.

diminished, their fears have vanished, but the burdensome obligations of christian morality remain before them.'[179]

But in spite of these reverses, the mission theocracies left a notable trace in the Ngangela region. It can be argued that they had saved the Ngangela from virtual extinction or absorption into more powerful neighbouring peoples, by providing security from raiders and by preserving and defending the Ngangela language. Moreover, mission influences persisted after the setbacks of the 1910s, although conversion rates were not as spectacular as in the Ovimbundu missions.[180] The Ngangela thus continued to have intermediaries between themselves and the colonial authorities, of a kind which the settler church of the highlands did not provide and which peoples without missionaries in the south-east did not enjoy.

The Wiko of south-eastern Angola were unable to resist the encroachments of their powerful neighbours, especially in the period between the 1880s and the 1910s, when the rubber boom suddenly made the region attractive. The Wiko were thus the victims of three types of encroachment. Firstly, they were threatened with progressive absorption into the Lozi empire of Barotseland on their eastern borders. Secondly, they were raided by peoples living to the north and south. Lastly, their territory was invaded by Cokwe and Luvale migrants from the north, who became active independent peasant producers. The Wiko themselves followed this example, and the most interesting feature of the history of this region was the way in which fairly intense petty commodity production did not disrupt the basic lineage structures of the social formations concerned, either among the original inhabitants or among the newcomers.

Complete absorption into the Lozi empire would have signified the entry into a fully feudal social formation, but this only occurred in a very few cases.[181] In the 1880s and 1890s, the Lozi consolidated their hold over small areas in the lower and middle Kwando valley.[182] There they imposed harsh demands for tribute, which were greatly resented.[183] But the Mashi of the Kwando marshes successfully resisted the imposition of Lozi control by force of arms, and their example was followed by others.[184] However, in general the Lozi were content to make alliances with the Wiko chiefs and headmen, whereby the Lozi could pasture their cattle in the flood season and in return would give military aid against

[179] AGCSSp, 476–B–V, Keiling to TRP 23/10/1911.
[180] *Annales Apostoliques*, XLV, 1, January 1929, pp. 18–25.
[181] Clarence-Smith, 1977b.
[182] Mainga, 1973, pp. 135–136; Stevenson-Hamilton, 1953, pp. 111–125, 197.
[183] Stevenson-Hamilton, 1953, p. 178.
[184] Stevenson-Hamilton, 1953, pp. 138, 148–150, 174, 185.

raiders.[185] Small gifts were sent by the Wiko chiefs concerned, but these payments in no way corresponded to the tribute paid by the serf population of the Lozi empire proper.[186] In addition, the 1905 boundary settlement between Northern Rhodesia and Angola made any further Lozi expansion impossible.[187]

The Wiko were subjected to frequent raids from the Okavango flood plain and from the north,[188] but more important was the steady flow of Cokwe and Luvale migrants during the rubber boom. The Cokwe managed to obtain control of a large proportion of rubber production, and they were especially prominent in Lucazi country, the heart of the rubber-producing areas.[189] Luvale immigrants specializing in rubber production were to be found further south, in the lands of the southern Mbunda.[190] But the various Wiko peoples also took to rubber production and began expanding into other people's lands.[191] In 1889, there were complaints of Lucazi and Mbunda invading the territory of a small tribe closely linked to the Lozi.[192] In short, the rubber boom set off complex movements of people searching for the precious root of the *carpodinus gracilis* plant, and there was probably a considerable rise in population.

The process of Cokwe expansion into north-east Angola has been analysed in depth, and scattered evidence for the south confirms this general picture.[193] The Cokwe moved in small groups, settling apart from local villages in densely wooded areas. They were submissive and cautious in their early relations with local inhabitants, and were generally welcomed as useful immigrants because of their skills in hunting, collecting, iron-working and medicine. Cokwe population expanded rapidly, as they bought up slave women and attracted local women to their villages. But the Cokwe never acquired feudal superstructures. Every village remained independent, based on a core of matrilineally related men with their numerous wives. Headmen exercised some control of trade in the village, but village fission was a frequent occurrence. Cokwe villages were united by a strong group consciousness, especially when it came to defending themselves against external threats, but they never developed any kind of centralized organization. However, as their numbers grew and as they

---

185 Gibbons, 1904, I, pp. 145, 226–227, 239, and II, p. 52; Portugal, 1903, part e, declaration of Consciencia.
186 *NAZ*, BS2/218, Harding, Report 16/1/1901; Clarence-Smith, 1977b.
187 Delgado, 1944, I, p. 493.
188 Gibbons, 1904, I, pp. 223–227; NAZ, BS2/159, Macaulay to Harding 23/6/1900.
189 NAZ, BS2/160, Harding, Report 4/7/1900.
190 Gibbons, 1904, I, p. 239.
191 NAZ, BS2/92, Lewanika to Worthington 3/10/1904; Gibbons, 1904, I, p. 266.
192 Gibbons, 1904, I, p. 251.
193 Miller, 1970, for process as a whole; Delachaux, 1948, pp. 13–15; NAZ, BS2/160, Harding, Report 4/7/1900; Vidal, 1912, pp. 464–465.

became well equipped with firearms, they became less submissive and began to raid their host societies.

The ending of the rubber boom in the early 1910s coincided with the imposition of colonial rule, and together these two phenomena led to a period of widespread violence and disorder. Many peasants found themselves in a desperate position, especially the Cokwe who depended most on rubber production.[194] As the price of rubber collapsed, the prices of imported articles rose because of inflation in Portugal, and colonial officials demanded the payment of hut tax.[195] Moreover, many peasants were deep in debt to European traders, and violence broke out when the latter attempted to reclaim their money.[196] Small rebellions occurred in various areas, and the Cokwe were additionally enraged by the fact that the republican authorities were stamping out the slave trade.[197] The peoples of the south-east therefore murdered traders, resisted tax-collectors and intensified the raiding of any neighbours weaker than themselves.[198]

Small military expeditions were mounted by the Portuguese to deal with this situation, but the peoples of the south-east proved an elusive foe. The vastness and remoteness of the region, the scattered population and the acephalous political organization of the tribes made it impossible to concentrate on one major objective. The Cokwe had also acquired a large stock of firearms during the ivory and rubber booms, and they were the moving force behind these rebellions.[199] Inconclusive campaigns thus continued well into the 1920s.[200]

The long-term results of the boom in rubber production in south-eastern Angola were that the peasantry was left in a particularly vulnerable position when the boom collapsed, so that migrant labour and permanent emigration became the rule. Labourers who went to the newly opened diamond fields in north-eastern Angola during the 1920s often became permanent emigrants, settling down in the peculiar 'state within a state' run by the DIAMANG company.[201] Migrant labour was also directed towards the Northern Rhodesian Copperbelt and the mines of South West Africa and South Africa.[202] Many Cokwe and Wiko also migrated to Barotseland and settled around the flood plain of the Upper Zambezi, although this was due more to problems of population pressure than to

---

[194] NAZ, BS2/160, Harding, Report 4/7/1900.
[195] AHM, 25P–16, Relatório da rebelião dos Luchazes 1917.
[196] NAZ, BS2/104, British Consul in Luanda to Foreign Secretary 8/8/1911.
[197] Pélissier, 1975, I, pp. 565–566; Delgado, 1940, pp. 341, 346.
[198] AGCSSp, 476–B–V, Keiling to TRP 4/2/1913 and 15/11/1916.
[199] AHM, 25P–16, Relatório da rebelião dos Luchazes 1917.
[200] Pélissier, 1975, I, pp. 574–575.
[201] *Africasia*, 3/1/1971, article on DIAMANG.
[202] Perrings, 1977; Galvão, 1930, pp. 237, 243.

the alleged comparative harshness of Portuguese colonial rule.[203] Lastly, Cokwe expansion and infiltration southwards continued, until they were checked by the resolute opposition of the peoples of the flood plains.[204]

The differing responses and the common destiny of the peasant societies of southern Angola reflect the uncertainties which characterized the period of colonial penetration. The process of transition from a series of autonomous lineage societies to a cluster of subject peasantries dependent on the colonial nucleus may seem with historical hindsight to have been inevitable and rapid. But the inevitability of the process was much less apparent to the people caught up in the complex, erratic and short-term changes of the period. This is especially true of the African peasants, who lacked any clear idea of the European background to the new forces impinging on their lives.

[203] Gluckman, 1968, p. 13; Pélissier, 1975, I, 949, n. 63.
[204] Delachaux, 1948, pp. 13–15.

7

Epilogue

The patterns of articulation between the colonial nucleus and African tributary societies established in the 1920s changed very little up to the 1950s, mainly because the economy of southern Angola stagnated during these decades. Military and administrative spending were cut back drastically after the final conquest of the Ovambo and the elimination of the German menace. This had a particularly severe effect on the economy of the Huíla highlands, which had depended to a very high degree on the market provided by the state.[1] Financial stringency became even more pronounced in the 1930s with the advent of Salazar, who insisted on a balanced budget and followed an extremely restrictive policy of public investment. Foreign investment was also strongly discouraged. Angola became a 'coffee economy', with subsidiary interests in the diamonds of the north-east and the Benguela railway.[2] The south was forgotten.[3]

The effects of the great depression of the late 1920s and early 1930s were also severely felt in southern Angola. Cotton production was hard hit, and cash crops ceased to play any significant role in the southern economy for two decades.[4] Exports of hides to Portugal remained fairly constant, but exports of live cattle declined. The quality of Angolan hides was very poor, and the share of the south in the rudimentary preparation of hides was much smaller than its share of the cattle population should have warranted. Wax from the south-east also continued to form a very small but fairly constant proportion of Angola's exports.[5]

The fishing industry, the main branch of production in the southern economy, was very adversely affected by the great depression. Thousands of kilos of rotten fish had to be thrown into the sea, and export figures

[1] Galvão, 1930, pp. 167–168, 269–270, 283.
[2] Wheeler and Pélissier, 1971, pp. 136–144.
[3] Santos, 1945, passim.
[4] Galvão, 1930, p. 177; *A Província de Angola*, 15/8/1965.
[5] Marques, 1964–1965, I, pp. 250–251, 255, 358–360.

remained low throughout the 1930s.[6] Recovery began after 1943, when the ban on motorized trawling in the Moçâmedes area was finally lifted and fish meal, fish oil and tinned fish found a better market in western Europe. But the industry remained bedevilled by archaic structures and was in a constant state of crisis. The main problem was that there were still very many small producers using rowing and sailing boats and employing very primitive methods in the preparation of dried fish. Indebtedness, undercapitalization and labour shortages compounded this problem, and the archaic structures of the industry became especially apparent when compared with developments in South West Africa and South Africa. Furthermore, Moçâmedes and neighbouring ports lost their overwhelming predominance in the Angolan fishing industry, although this part of the coast continued to account for over half the annual catch. Lobito and other ports in that area emerged as important competitors, favoured by the completion of the Benguela railway, which facilitated sales of dried fish in central Angola and in Katanga.[7]

Supplies of cheap migrant labour remained the key to the economy of southern Angola, but employers had to face strong competition from South West Africa. Salaries and conditions were generally better in South West Africa, although average salaries in the Moçâmedes fisheries in the 1950s were apparently slightly above the minimum wage paid in South West Africa. A high degree of administrative compulsion thus continued to be used to mobilize labour, especially in the form of unpaid or badly paid forced labour on public works. Migrant labourers brought back thousands of pounds from South West Africa every year, but attempts to profit from this situation by increasing taxation were counter-productive, leading to large-scale migration of Ovambo and Kwangali over the border.[8]

Economic stagnation was matched by a lack of conspicuous changes in either the colonial nucleus or African tributary societies, although a great deal more research in this field is needed. New white settlement was on a small scale. The lands abandoned by the Boers in 1928 were filled by a slow trickle of spontaneous immigration from northern Portugal, and new farms were created to the north-east of Lubango after the Second World War.[9] In 1953, a *colonato* (state colonization scheme) was set up on the middle Cunene by the new Matala dam, and about 300 families were installed in what had previously been very sparsely populated terri-

[6] Azevedo, 1945, p. 144; Cya, 1936, pp. 111–113; Marques, 1964–1965, I, pp. 402, 421.
[7] Marques, 1964–1965, I, pp. 395–426; Nascimento and Silva, 1959; Santos, 1945, pp. 143–145.
[8] Mendes, 1958, pp. 95, 144; Machado, 1956, p. 441; Neto, 1963, pp. 208–209.
[9] Medeiros, 1976, pp. 277–287.

tory.[10] But even in 1960, there were still only just over 25,000 whites in all of southern Angola.[11] In the 1940s, southern whites were described as a backward and conservative community, which still included a high proportion of poor families, who lacked either land or fishing boats.[12]

African tributary societies in the south were also noted for their conservative attitude and lack of socio-economic development.[13] Expenditure on social infrastructures was low all over Angola in the Salazarist era,[14] but this seems to have been particularly marked in the remote south.[15] Towns were small and stagnant, and their non-white population was chiefly made up of Kimbari and Africans from other parts of Angola.[16] Changes were greatest in the flood plains, where increasing population pressure on limited resources resulted in a particularly high rate of migrant labour.[17] Conversions to christianity and outward signs of western cultural influence were thus most notable in this region, whereas the peoples of the highlands became famous for their cultural conservatism.[18]

The sleepy and forgotten south began to stir in the 1950s, but rapid social and economic changes did not occur until the insurrection of 1961 in northern Angola and the subsequent liberation struggle. The great majority of the people in the south was not directly involved in the fighting, although the sparsely populated plains of the south-east did become a battle-ground in the late 1960s.[19] But the Portuguese authorities were fearful of new explosions of peasant violence after 1961, and they therefore began a general campaign to 'win hearts and minds'. Ovamboland was considered a particularly dangerous area, both because of its complex economic problems and because of 'subversive influences' coming from the neighbouring Ovambo Bantustan.[20] In addition to government measures to alleviate peasant grievances, there occurred a major economic boom in Angola, as state expenditure multiplied, foreign investment was encouraged and world markets remained buoyant.[21]

The south was thus caught up in the general process of economic growth and social ameliorations which spread through Angola. Spending on health and education increased and forced labour was abolished in 1962. Communications improved dramatically, with the extension and reconstruction of the Moçâmedes railway, the building of a new port in Moçâmedes harbour, the laying down of an excellent network of tarred

[10] Kuder, 1971, p. 67; Chapman, 1971, p. 30.
[11] Angola, 1964, I.
[12] Santos, 1945, p. 179 and passim; Guimarães and Paiva, 1942, p. 35.
[13] Silva, 1978.   [14] Wheeler and Pélissier, 1971, p. 142.
[15] Silva, 1978.
[16] Estermann, 1939; Medeiros, 1976, p. 572.   [17] Moorsom, 1977.
[18] Silva, 1978.   [19] Davidson, 1972, pp. 17–44; Bender, 1978, pp. 170–179.
[20] Silva, 1978; Bender, 1978, passim.
[21] Wheeler and Pélissier, 1971, chapters 9 and 10.

roads and the spread of airfields. Cheap hydroelectricity from the new Matala dam on the Cunene progressively reached the main towns and centres of economic activity. Foreign investment was most obviously apparent in the Cassinga iron mines, but also became involved in fishing and ranching. White settlers surged into the area again, being particularly attracted by the booming town of Lubango (then Sá da Bandeira). Finally, an ambitious and expensive plan for hydroelectricity, irrigated farming and scientific cattle ranching in the entire Cunene valley was launched in the late 1960s, in close association with the South African government.[22]

The 1960s were a decade of expansion and modernization for the southern fisheries, stimulated by government aid, foreign investment and a generally satisfactory world market. Fish meal became by far the most valuable export of the Angolan fisheries, worth more than twice all other fish products put together in 1969. Exports of tinned fish, fish oil and frozen fish all grew, although dried fish for local African markets remained the second most valuable product. The number of motorized vessels increased and several new factories were built. Nevertheless, the structural problems of the fishing industry were by no means entirely resolved. The instability of external markets and the persistence of small archaic productive units continued to dog the industry and to make for only modest overall progress.[23]

Economic growth in the interior was stimulated first and foremost by the amelioration of communications. The tarred roads were laid down largely for strategic reasons and the railway was rebuilt to serve the Cassinga iron mines, but both of these improvements had considerable economic side-effects. Most significant was the rapid development of maize exports from areas along the line of rail. By 1969, 42% of Angola's maize exports came from the south, whereas ten years earlier exports had been negligible. The railway also stimulated timber production in the south-east and the quarrying of marble in the vicinity of Moçâmedes. Railway and roads were vital for the success of the Matala *colonato*, which grew wheat, maize, tobacco and tomatoes, and had small factories for processing the latter two commodities.[24]

Other sectors of the economy grew more in response to high market prices, although the importance of improved communications cannot be overstressed. The coastal oases specialized in fruit production, especially olives, as food for the labour force in the fisheries was now provided by

22 Kuder, 1971, passim; Silva, 1978; see map 4, p. 108.
23 Kuder, 1971, pp. 104–107, 233–236; Chapman, 1971, pp. 34, 45, 49–50.
24 Kuder, 1971, pp. 88, 129, 138 n.23 (maize), 102 (wood), 114 (marble), 67 (Matala).

maize from the interior. The plantations of the foothills, which had often been abandoned since the collapse of cotton prices in the 1930s, were reoccupied and entered into a new era of prosperity, with the introduction of tobacco and sisal as new cash crops. Tobacco was more important in southern areas, whereas sisal predominated to the north in the hinterland of Lobito.[25] However, cotton increasingly replaced sisal in the late 1960s, as sisal prices fell on the world market.[26] The 1960s also witnessed a revival of interest in the pastoral potential of southern Angola. Dairy and beef freezing plants became more numerous in Lubango and Moçâmedes. There was also an attempt to reactivate the raising of Karakul sheep for lambs' pelts in the Namib desert, but this scheme met with only limited success. Efforts were made to raise the quality and quantity of cattle products in the African peasant sector, mainly by providing water, but also by vaccination and cross-breeding. In general terms, however, growth in the pastoral field remained below expectations.[27]

The third focus for economic growth in the interior was the rapid development of the town of Lubango (then Sá da Bandeira), which was declared a zone of first priority for industrialization.[28] The population of the town doubled between 1960 and 1970, reaching a total of just over 30,000 inhabitants. Flour milling, meat freezing and other processing of agricultural production did develop, but the rapid growth of the town was due rather to greatly increased military and administrative expenditure, a situation in many ways reminiscent of the 1900s and 1910s. The town also became a focal point for the expansion of market gardening in the Huíla highlands, which began to supply the booming city of Luanda as well. Finally, Lubango became an important centre for railway maintenance and road transport, and the Huíla highlands attracted a modest but increasing flow of tourists from South Africa and South West Africa.[29]

The prosperity of the 1960s and early 1970s resulted in a number of changes in the societies of southern Angola. The colonial nucleus expanded considerably, both in terms of numbers and in terms of the geographical areas included within it. The new plantations, farms and ranches, the Cassinga iron mines, and the new urban centres which sprang up along the line of rail and the tarred roads were all characterized by wage labour and production for the market. The sharp differentiation between capitalist and pre-capitalist sectors became more blurred in areas like the Huíla highlands, where an African cash cropping peasantry

[25] *A Província de Angola*, 15/8/1964 and 15/8/1965; Kuder, 1971, pp. 83–85, 91.
[26] Chapman, 1971, p. 29; Kuder, 1971, p. 87.
[27] Kuder, 1971, pp. 93–101; Chapman, 1971, p. 48; *A Província de Angola*, 15/8/1964 and 15/8/1965.
[28] Chapman, 1971, p. 46.   [29] Medeiros, 1976, pp. 603–611.

developed. Finally, the poor white problem appears to have been dealt with during this decade.[30]

African peasant societies became more closely dominated and controlled by the colonial nucleus, losing both land and some of the political and social autonomy which had been left to them since the 1920s. The network of administrative posts, schools and clinics became denser or was established where it had scarcely existed before, and the position of chiefs was further eroded.[31] Efforts were also made to sedentarize transhumant pastors in order to control them better, especially the semi-nomadic Herero tribes.[32] Land alienation became a problem once again, especially in the tobacco and sisal lands below the escarpment and in the ranch lands of the south-west.[33] An official survey of the early 1970s indicated that land alienation was not a major preoccupation for African peasants, but one clearly has to be wary of answers given to officials in an extremely authoritarian political system.[34] Medeiros reported considerable bitterness at land alienation in private conversations with educated and articulate Africans, contrasting with statements in more public and official situations.[35] It should also be noted that concern at land alienation was to be seen against a background of increasing population pressure on resources in both Ovamboland and the Huíla highlands. Furthermore, the fencing of ranches led to grave disruptions in the patterns of transhumance which were vital to African cattle raisers.[36]

The closer integration of African peasants into capitalist relations of production was mainly achieved through an intensification of migrant labour, although it must be stressed that this integration was still very far from complete. After the abolition of forced labour in 1962, a much higher level of taxation was introduced, which served as an alternative 'stimulant' to migrant labour.[37] Moreover, the crisis in subsistence production in Ovamboland was becoming ever more severe in the 1960s. This problem has been studied in the more arid and overcrowded South African sector, but there were also reports of soil erosion and excessive deforestation to the north of the frontier, especially in the territory of the key Kwanyama tribe.[38] Population pressure was becoming severe in the Huíla highlands as well in the 1960s, leading to very high rates of migrant labour and to an urban drift into Lubango.[39] The fisheries of the Angolan coast and the mines and fisheries of South West Africa continued to be the

[30] Medeiros, 1976, pp. 603–611.   [31] Silva, 1978; Neto, 1963, p. 107.
[32] *A Província de Angola*, 15/8/1964 and 15/8/1965; Bender, 1978, pp. 188–194.
[33] Medeiros, 1976, pp. 400, 423–424, 524; Hauenstein, 1967, p. 3.
[34] Heimer, 1972, tables 65–68, 135–136.   [35] Medeiros, 1976, pp. 423–424.
[36] Silva, 1978; Moorsom, 1977; Carvalho and Silva, 1973.
[37] Neto, 1963, pp. 203–204; Medeiros, 1976, p. 528.
[38] Moorsom, 1977; Machado, 1956, pp. 446–447; Neto, 1963, pp. 21–22.
[39] Silva, 1978.

main centres of employment, but Lubango, Luanda and the coffee lands of northern Angola were also significant places of employment for southern labour. Wages increased slightly, but both wages and conditions remained very poor.[40]

At the same time, there was a considerable growth in the amounts of cash crops or cattle produced by peasants for the market. Most of the maize exported from southern Angola was low quality produce grown by African peasants, although tobacco, cotton and sisal were mainly plantation crops.[41] Improved production methods, including ploughs and irrigation, spread among the Nyaneka, in spite of their reputation as a hopelessly backward and conservative people.[42] The great bulk of cattle raising also remained in African hands, serving mainly the corned beef factories and the trade in hides. The setting up of rural markets and the increased level of taxation had some effect in increasing sales of cattle by Africans, although much less than had been hoped in official circles.[43]

Increased petty commodity production may have been responsible for a development of social stratification in African peasant societies, although it is totally unclear how much this was merely a relic from earlier periods of class formation.[44] At any rate, in both the Huíla highlands and the flood plains, there were reports of wealthy cattle owners employing poor pastors who owned no cattle on fairly exploitative terms.[45] In Ovamboland, poor pastors tended not to be able to marry, and thus to have a very insufficient crop production, whereas wealthy cattle owners had many wives and consequently a large crop production. But the majority of the population appears to have fallen into the category of monogamous 'middle peasants', owning an average of twenty head of cattle, which were tended entirely by family labour. Unfortunately, Lima does not provide any numerical indications as to the relative size of these social groups.[46]

The economic boom in the south was brought to an abrupt conclusion after 1974. The area became a battle-ground, as the forces of the different liberation groups and their foreign allies swept backwards and forwards, often destroying and looting much valuable material in the process.[47] Many white settlers fled, breaking or damaging more vital equipment as

[40] Medeiros, 1976, pp. 381, 573–576; Bender, 1978, p. 226, n. 45.
[41] Kuder, 1971, p. 88 and passim.
[42] Medeiros, 1976, pp. 346–348, 449–450.
[43] Kuder, 1971, pp. 93–101; Neto, 1963, p. 71; Medeiros, 1976, pp. 527–528; *A Província de Angola*, 15/8/1964.
[44] See chapter 6, pp. 74–82 for earlier days in the Ovambo case; Lang and Tastevin, 1937, p. 86 for the Nyaneka.
[45] Lima, 1977, pp. 125–129; Medeiros, 1976, pp. 462–463.
[46] Lima, 1977, pp. 125–129.
[47] *Angola Solidarity Committee News*, 2–7, 1975–1976.

they left and depriving the area of skilled personnel.[48] Nor were the troubles of the south over with the victory of the MPLA in 1976. UNITA continued guerilla operations in south-eastern Angola, with the logistic backing of the South African army, and the threat of South African hot pursuit of SWAPO guerillas continued to hang over the area.[49] Moreover, Ovambo separatism was encouraged by South African plans for the independence of a 'Greater Owambo'.[50] The restoration of peace and prosperity thus depends closely on political developments in South West Africa.

Nevertheless, the shattered southern economy did begin to recover slowly after the final victory of the MPLA in the south-west in early 1976. By about September of that year, the railway had resumed services between Moçâmedes and the interior, and the work of repairing roads and bridges had begun. Moçâmedes port was handling a certain amount of fish, meat and vegetables for the desperately short markets in Luanda and northern Angola, but the Cassinga iron mines had not resumed operations. Fish production was still on a very small scale and limited largely to dried fish. Equipment for more complex fish products had either been destroyed or was unusable for lack of qualified personnel. Venancio Guimarães had fled the country, and his various plantations, ranches and food-processing plants had been taken over by MPLA cadres and were slowly being put back into production. The Cunene valley project was at a standstill and the Angolan government was speaking of radical future modifications in the plan, which had been conceived to serve mainly South African interests.[51] Here again, future developments in South West Africa are of crucial importance to southern Angola.

[48] *Angola Solidarity Committee News*, 6, February 1976, pp. 5, and 13, October 1976, pp. 5–6.
[49] Fauvet, 1977, pp. 44–45.
[50] Heimer, 1976, p. 56.
[51] *Angola Solidarity Committee News*, 13, October 1976, pp. 2–3, 5–7.

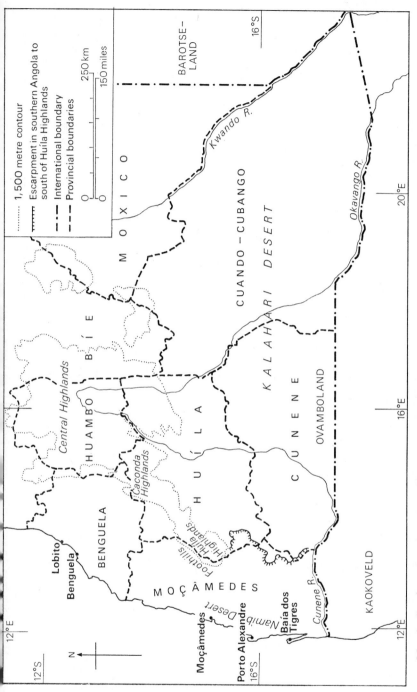

Map 1 Southern Angola – physical features (adapted from Kuder, 1971)

Legend:
..... 1,500 metre contour
Escarpment in southern Angola to south of Huíla Highlands
–··– International boundary
––– Provincial boundaries

0   250 km
0   150 miles

16°S

BAROTSE-LAND

MOXICO

Kwando R.

20°E

CUANDO – CUBANGO

KALAHARI DESERT

Okavango R.

BÍE

Central Highlands

HUAMBO

Caconda Highlands

HUÍLA

Foothills

Huíla Highlands

CUNENE

CUNENE

OVAMBOLAND

16°E

BENGUELA

Lobito
Benguela

MOÇÂMEDES

Moçâmedes

Namib Desert

Porto Alexandre

Baía dos Tigres

Cunene R.

KAOKOVELD

12°E

12°E

12°S

16°S

N

105

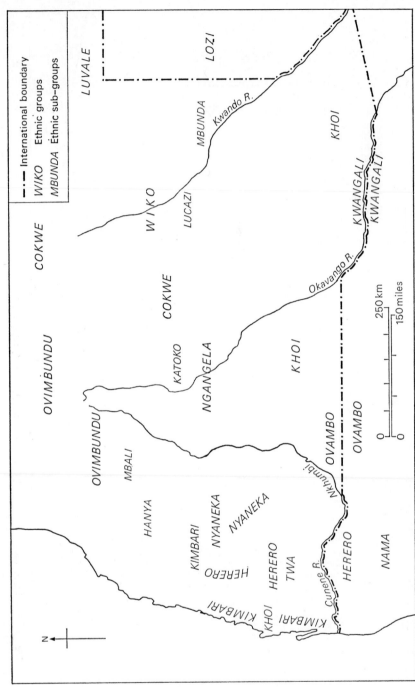

Map 2 Southern Angola – ethnic groups (adapted from Kuder, 1971)

106

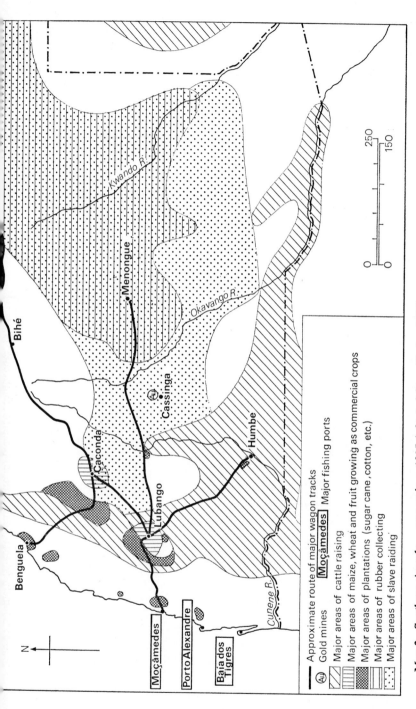

Map 3 Southern Angola – economic c. 1905 (adapted from Kuder, 1971)

Legend:
- Approximate route of major wagon tracks
- Ⓐ Gold mines   Moçâmedes Major fishing ports
- Major areas of cattle raising
- Major areas of maize, wheat and fruit growing as commercial crops
- Major areas of plantations (sugar cane, cotton, etc.)
- Major areas of rubber collecting
- Major areas of slave raiding

Place names: Benguela, Bihé, Kwando R., Menongue, Okavango R., Cassinga, Caconda, Lubango, Humbe, Cunene R., Moçâmedes, Porto Alexandre, Baía dos Tigres

Scale: 0 — 150 — 250

N

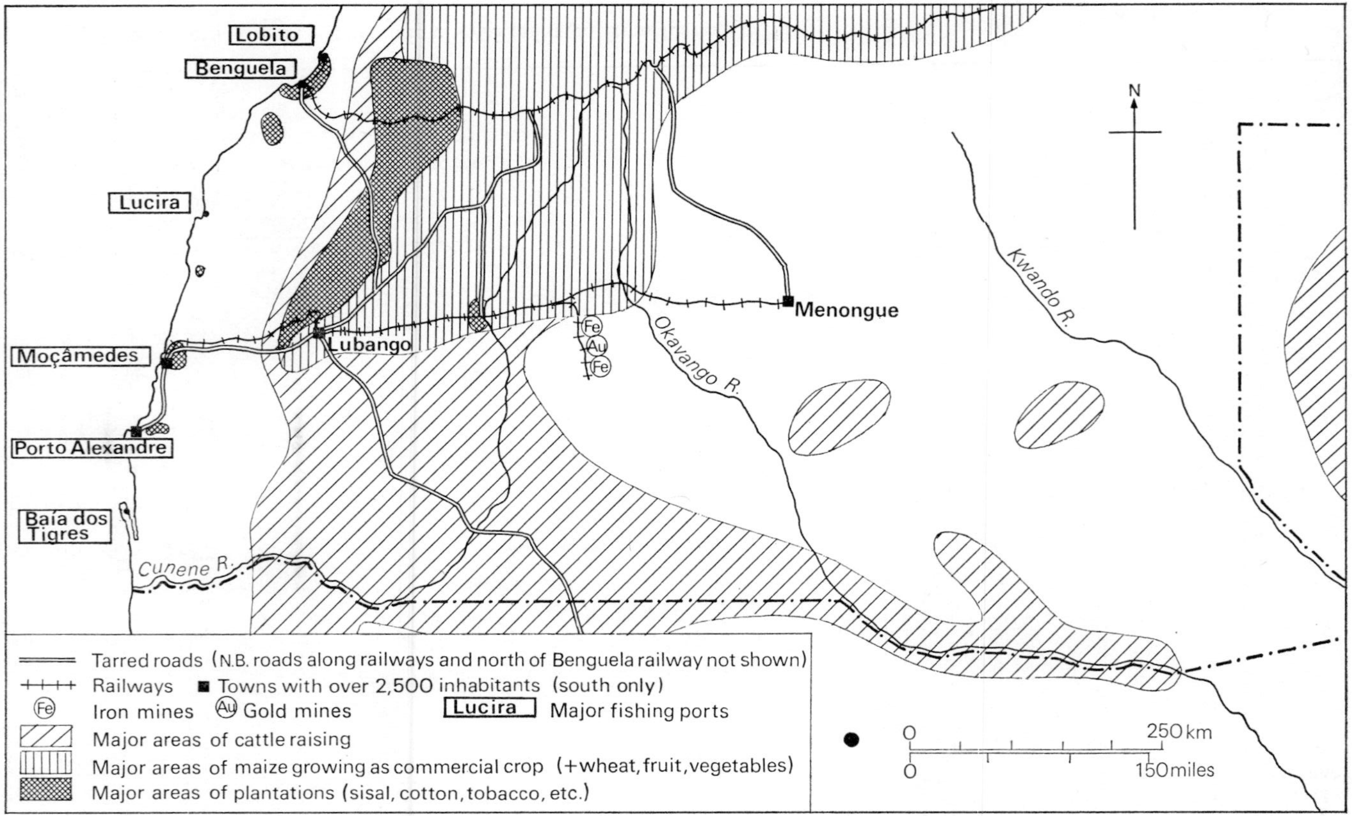

Map 4 Southern Angola – economic c. 1970 (adapted from Kuder, 1971)

Legend:

Tarred roads (N.B. roads along railways and north of Benguela railway not shown)
+++ Railways
(Fe) Iron mines (Au) Gold mines
Towns with over 2,500 inhabitants (south only) Lucira Major fishing ports
Lucira (+wheat, fruit, vegetables)
Major areas of cattle raising
Major areas of maize growing as commercial crop
Major areas of plantations (sisal, cotton, tobacco, etc.)

Labels on map: Kwando R., Menongue, Okavango R., Lubango, Lobito, Benguela, Lucira, Moçâmedes, Porto Alexandre, Baía dos Tigres, Cunene R.

250 km
150 miles

108

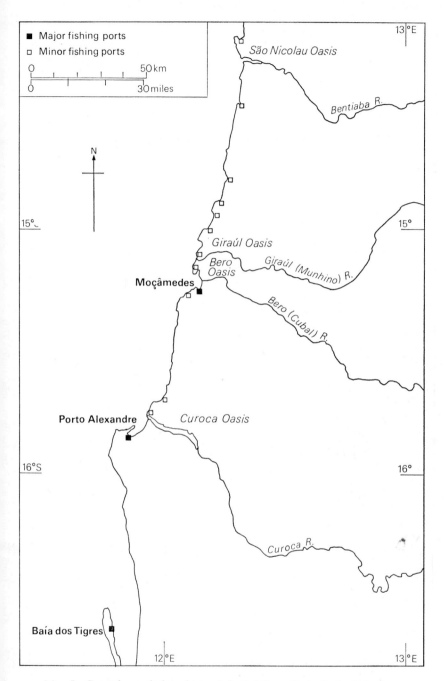

Map 5 Coastal population cluster (adapted from Carta Rodoviária de
Angola, Junta Autónoma das Estradas de Angola, 1969/1970)
Note: All rivers dry for most months of the year

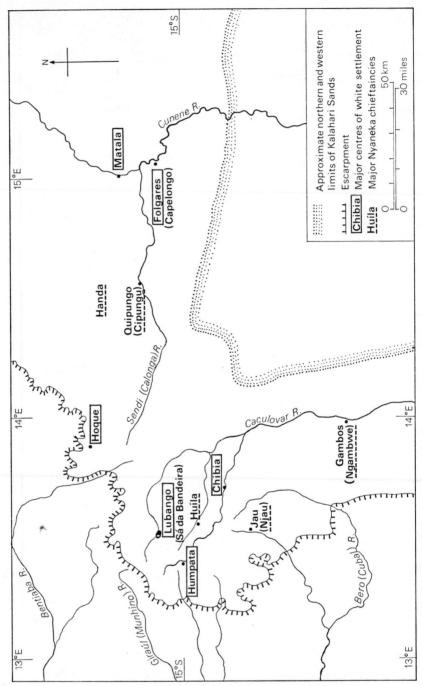

Map 6 Nyaneka population cluster (adapted from Carta Rodoviária de Angola, Junta Autónoma das Estradas de Angola, 1969/1970)

Legend:
- Approximate northern and western limits of Kalahari Sands
- Escarpment
- Chibia Major centres of white settlement
- Huíla Major Nyaneka chieftaincies

Places:
- Matala
- Folgares (Capelongo)
- Handa
- Quipungo (Cipungu)
- Hoque
- Lubango (Sá da Bandeira)
- Huíla
- Chibia
- Humpata
- Jau (Njau)
- Gambos (Ngambwe)

Rivers:
- Cunene R.
- Sendi (Calonga) R.
- Caculovar R.
- Bentiaba R.
- Giraúl (Munhino) R.
- Bero (Cubal) R.

110

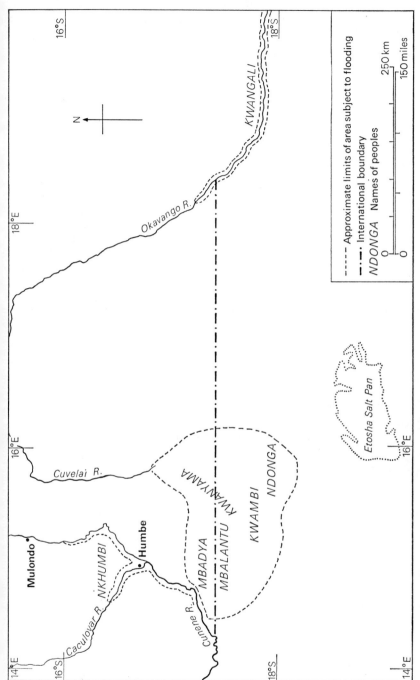

Map 7 The flood plains (adapted from Map 3928, Cuvelai River Basin; South West African Administration, Water Affairs Branch)

111

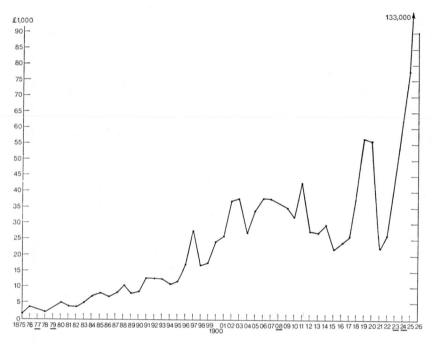

Graph 1 Exports of fish products through Moçâmedes and its fiscal dependencies, 1875–1926. No information for years underlined

112

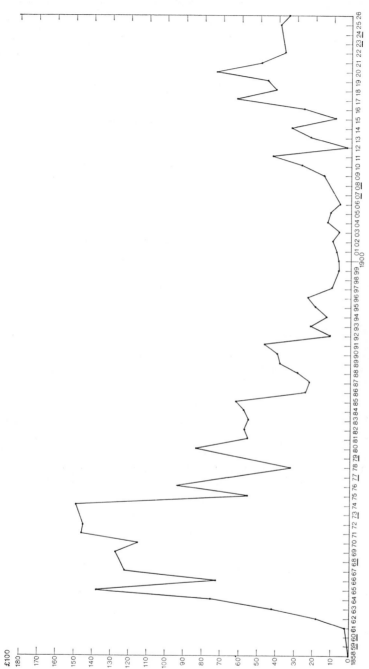

£100

Graph 2   Exports of raw cotton through Moçâmedes and its fiscal
dependencies, 1858–1926. No information for years underlined

113

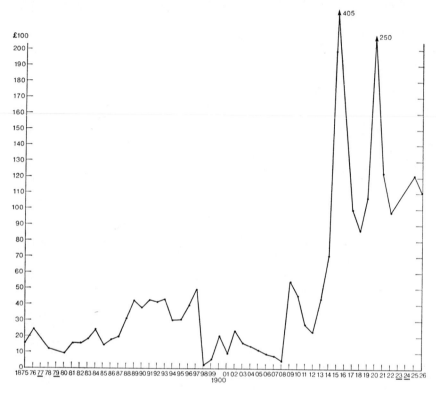

Graph 3 Exports of cattle products through Moçâmedes and its fiscal
dependencies, 1875–1926. No information for years underlined

114

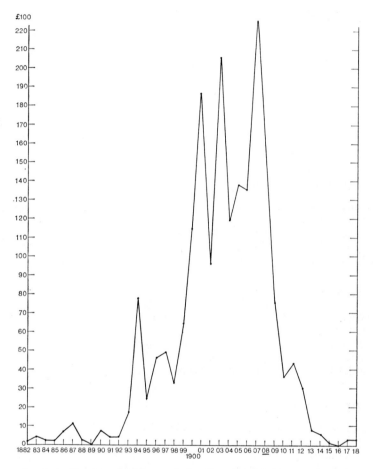

Graph 4 Exports of rubber and *almeidina* through Moçâmedes and its fiscal dependencies, 1882–1918. No information for year underlined

Sources and bibliography

ARCHIVAL SOURCES

I Portuguese Archives

- Arquivo Histórico Ultramarino, Lisboa. (Segunda Secção: Correspondência dos Governadores Gerais de Angola, Repartições 1, 2, e 4; Companhia de Moçâmedes; Alfândegas.)
- Arquivo Histórico Militar, Lisboa. (Segunda Secção, Segunda Divisão. All classifications provisional.)

II Other European Archives

- Archives Générales de la Congrégation du Saint-Esprit, Paris. (Cunène et Cimbébasie.)
- Archives du Ministère des Affaires Etrangères, Paris.
- Public Record Office, London.
- Rhodes Papers, Rhodes House, Oxford.

III Angolan Archives

- Arquivo Histórico de Angola, Luanda. (Avulsos e Códices.)
- Arquivo Histórico do Museu da Huíla, Lubango. (All classifications provisional.)

IV Other African Archives

- National Archives of Zambia, Lusaka.
- Livingstone Museum Manuscript Collection, Livingstone.
- Staatsargief, Pretoria.
- Witwatersrand University Archives, Johannesburg. (Damaraland Diocesan Records. Photocopies courtesy of Richard Moorsom.)

Note: Further details on sections I, II and III are to be found in Clarence-Smith, 1975, pp. 18–21, 427–430, including some minor archival sources not used for this study.

116

SERIAL SOURCES

Angola Solidarity Committee News, London.
Annales Apostoliques, Paris.
Annual Series, London (Foreign Office).
Boletim da Sociedade de Geografia de Lisboa, Lisboa.
Boletim Official, Luanda.
Bulletin Général, Paris (Congrégation du Saint-Esprit).
Commercio de Mossamedes, Moçâmedes.
Correio de Mossamedes, Moçâmedes.
Estatística Commercial, Luanda.
Grande Enciclopédia Portuguesa e Brasileira, Lisboa and Rio de Janeiro.
Jornal de Mossamedes, Moçâmedes.
Journal des Missions Evangéliques, Paris.
Parliamentary Papers, London.
Philafricain, Le, Lausanne.
Portugal em Africa, Lisboa.
Sul, O, Moçâmedes.

SOURCES FOR CUSTOMS STATISTICS

Note: The best series are to be found in the *Boletim Oficial* and in
      Estatística Commercial.

AHU, Alfândegas, and scattered documents.
AHA, Cod–G(3)–4–1, Cod–(4)–1–1, and scattered documents.
Annual Series, various years.
Boletim das Alfândegas da Província de Angola, 8, August 1924.
Boletim Oficial, various years, especially in appendices.
Estatística Commercial, Luanda, from 1909.
Parliamentary Papers (Great Britain), Consular Reports, various years.
Angola, 1901, quadro 5.
Araujo, 1900, pp. 137–140.
Couceiro, 1910, passim.
Felner, 1940, II, pp. 264–265.
Silva, 1971–1973, 34, pp. 508–511.
Torres, 1950, pp. 364–365, 435–466.
Torres, 1952, pp. 51–52.

SOURCES FOR EXCHANGE RATES
OF PORTUGUESE CURRENCY

Note: The best series are to be found in *Annual Series* and in Marques
      1973.

Archives du Ministère des Affaires Etrangères, Paris, scattered references
Annual Series, various years.
Parliamentary Papers (Great Britain), Consular Reports, various years.
Duparquet, 1953, p. 162.
Livingstone, 1963, I, p. 200.
Marques, 1973, pp. 206–208.

Marvaud, 1912, p. 89.
Menezes, 1867, pp. 25, 120–122.
Möller, 1974, p. 12.
Samuels, 1970, p. 169.
Teixeira, 1934, p. 378.

SELECT BIBLIOGRAPHY

Note: The bibliography is limited to works cited in text and notes.

Almeida, José Bento Ferreira de, 1880, *Mossamedes*, Lisboa.
Almeida, João de, 1912, *Sul d'Angola, relatório de um governo de distrito, 1908–1910*, Lisboa.
Alves, Carlos Martins e Castro, 1970, 'Bernardino Freire de Figueiredo Abreu e Castro, bosquejo biográfico do colonizador de Moçâmedes', Dissertação de Licenciatura, Instituto Superior de Ciências Sociais e Política Ultramarina, Universidade Técnica de Lisboa (also published in *Garcia de Orta*, XVIII, 1–4, 1970).
Amaral, Francisco Joaquim Ferreira do, 1880, *As colónias agrícolas em Africa e a lei*, Lisboa.
Andersson, Charles John, 1856, *Lake Ngami*, London.
Andersson, Charles John, 1875, *Notes of travel in South Africa*, London.
Angebauer, Karl, 1927, *Ovambo, fünfzehn Jahre unter Kaffern, Buschleuten und Bezirksamtmännern*, Berlin.
Angola, Governo Geral, 1901, *Annuário estatístico da província de Angola*, Luanda.
Angola, Repartição do Gabinete, 1910, *Relatório da missão de colonização no planalto de Benguela em 1909*, Luanda.
Angola, Direção dos Serviços de Economia e Estatística Geral, 1964, *Terceiro recenseamento geral da população, 1960*, Luanda.
Araujo, António José de, 1900, *Les colonies portugaises d'Afrique*, Lisboa.
Axelson, Eric, 1967, *Portugal and the scramble for Africa*, Johannesburg.
Axelson, Eric, 1973, *Congo to Cape, early Portuguese explorers*, London.
Azevedo, João Maria Cerqueira de, 1945, *Subsídios para o estudo da economia de Angola nos últimos cem anos*, no place of publication.
Azevedo, João Maria Cerqueira de, 1958, *Angola, exemplo de trabalho*, Luanda.
Barns, T. A., 1928, *Angolan sketches*, London.
Bender, Gerald J., 1978, *Angola under the Portuguese, the myth and the reality*, London.
Bley, Helmut, 1971, *South West Africa under German rule, 1894–1914*, London.
Borchert, Günter, 1963, *Südost-Angola, Landschaft, Landschaftshaushalt und Entwicklungsmöglichkeiten im Vergleich zum zentralen Hochland von Mittelangola*, Hamburg.
Botelho, Eduardo Rodrigues Vieira da Costa, 1890, 'Relatório, 29/5/1889', in *Boletim Oficial*, 1890 *apensos*.
Brásio, António, 1966–1971, *Angola*, Pittsburgh and Louvain, 5 volumes.

Braz, Cesar de Oliveira Moura, 1918, *Distrito da Huíla, relatório do governador, ano de 1912*, Coimbra.

Brochado, Bernardino José, 1855, 'Descripção das terras do Humbe, Camba, Mulondo, Quanhama e outras' and 'Notícia de alguns territórios, e dos povos que os habitam, situados na parte meridional da província de Angola', *Annaes do Conselho Ultramarino*, parte não-oficial, primeira série, November and December, pp. 187–197 and 203–208.

Bullock, G. H., 1932, *Economic conditions in Angola (Portuguese West Africa)*, London (Department of Overseas Trade).

Cabral, Manuel Villaverde, 1977, *O desenvolvimento do capitalismo em Portugal no século XIX*, Lisboa, second edition.

Capela, José, 1975, *A burguesia mercantil do Porto e as colónias, 1834–1900*, Porto.

Capela, José, 1977, *O imposto de palhota e a introdução do modo de produção capitalista nas colónias*, Porto.

Capello, Hermenegildo, and Ivens, Roberto, 1886, *De Angola à contra-costa*, Lisboa, 2 volumes.

Caraman, Philip, 1975, *The lost paradise, an account of the Jesuits in Paraguay, 1607–1768*, London.

Cardoso, Carlos Lopes, 1966, 'Olumbali no distrito de Moçâmedes', in *Boletim do Instituto de Investigação Científica de Angola*, 3, 1, pp. 37–73.

Carneiro, Carlos Baptista, 1934, *Conservas de peixe*, Luanda.

Carvalho, Eduardo Cruz de, and Silva, Jorge Vieira da, 1973, 'The Cunene region, ecological analysis of an African agropastoral system', in F. W. Heimer (ed.) *Social change in Angola*, München, pp. 145–192.

Carvalho, Filipe Carlos Dias de, 1904, 'Apontamentos d'uma viagem no sul d'Angola', in *Boletim da Sociedade de Geografia de Lisboa*, XXII, 2 to 4, pp. 33–44, 65–77, 126–134.

Carvalho, Tito Augusto de, 1900, *Les colonies portugaises au point de vue commercial*, Paris and Lisboa.

Castilho, Augusto de, 1899, 'As bahias do sul de Angola', in *Portugal em Africa*, 63 to 65, March to May, pp. 129–140, 177–188, 233–239.

Castro, José Velloso de, 1908, *A campanha do Cuamato em 1907*, Luanda.

Chapman, Michael, 1971, *Angola on the road to progress*, Luanda.

Chatelain, Alida, 1918, *Héli Chatelain, l'ami de l'Angola, 1859–1908*, Lausanne.

Childs, Gladwyn Murray, 1969, *Kinship and character of the Ovimbundu*, London.

Cid, Francisco de Paula, 1894, *Relatório do governador do distrito de Benguella, 1892*, Lisboa (Ministério da Marinha e do Ultramar).

Clarence-Smith, William Gervase, 1974, 'Drought in southern Angola and northern Namibia, 1837–1945', unpublished paper, SOAS African History Seminar, University of London.

Clarence-Smith, William Gervase, 1975, 'Mossamedes and its hinterland, 1875–1915', Ph.D. Thesis, University of London.

Clarence-Smith, William Gervase, 1976 a, 'Slavery in coastal southern

Angola, 1875–1913', *Journal of Southern African Studies*, II, 2, pp. 214–223.

Clarence-Smith, William Gervase, 1976 b, 'The Thirstland Trekkers in Angola', *The Societies of Southern Africa in the 19th and 20th Centuries*, VI, pp. 42–51.

Clarence-Smith, William Gervase, 1977 a, 'For Braudel: A note on the Ecole des Annales and the historiography of Africa', *History in Africa*, IV, pp. 275–281.

Clarence-Smith, William Gervase, 1977 b, 'The Lozi social formation, 1875–1906', History Seminars, University of Zambia, Lusaka (revised version, 'Slaves, Commoners and Landlords in Bulozi *c*. 1875–1906', *Journal of African History*, XX, 2, 1979).

Clarence-Smith, William Gervase, and Moorsom, Richard, 1975, 'Underdevelopment and class formation in Ovamboland, 1845–1915', *Journal of African History*, XVI, 3, 1975, pp. 365–381.

Clarence-Smith, William Gervase, and Moorsom, Richard, 1977, 'Underdevelopment and class formation in Ovamboland, 1844–1917', *The roots of rural poverty in central and southern Africa*, R. Palmer and Q. N. Parsons (eds.), London, pp. 96–112.

Contreiras, Manoel José Martins, 1894, *A província de Angola, breves considerações sobre o seu presente e futuro administrativo, agrícola, commercial e financeiro*, Lisboa.

Couceiro, Henrique Mitchell de Paiva, 1910, *Angola, dous annos de governo, junho 1907–junho 1909*, Lisboa.

Coutinho, João de Azevedo, 1910, *A questão do alcool de Angola, proposta de lei*, Lisboa (Ministério da Marinha e do Ultramar).

Cya, Carlo, 1936, *Economia affricana, le colonie portoghesi*, Firenze.

Davidson, Basil, 1972, *In the eye of the storm, Angola's people*, London.

Delachaux, Théodore, 1948, *Ethnographie de la région du Cunène*, Neuchâtel (also published in *Bulletin de la Société Neuchâteloise de Géographie*, XLIV, 2, 1936, pp. 5–108).

Delgado, Ralph, 1940, *A famosa e histórica Benguela, catálogo dos governadores 1779–1940*, Lisboa.

Delgado, Ralph, 1944, *Ao sul do Cuanza, ocupação e aproveitamento do antigo reino de Benguela, 1483–1942*, Lisboa.

Deutschland, Reichskolonialamt, 1910 and 1911, *Die deutschen Schutzgebiete in Afrika und der Südsee, amtliche Jahresberichte*, Berlin.

Dias, Gastão Sousa, 1923, *No planalto da Huíla*, Porto.

Dias, Gastão Sousa, 1943, *Os auxiliares na ocupação do sul de Angola*, Lisboa (Agência Geral das Colónias, Coleção Pelo Império, 96).

Diniz, José de Oliveira Ferreira, 1914, *Negócios indígenas, relatório do ano de 1913*, Luanda.

Diniz, José de Oliveira Ferreira, 1915, *Negócios indígenas, relatório do ano de 1914*, Luanda.

Diniz, José de Oliveira Ferreira, 1917, *Negócios indígenas, relatório do ano de 1916*, Lisboa.

Drechsler, Horst, 1962, 'L'Allemagne et l'Angola du Sud, 1898–1903', in *Présence Africaine*, 42, pp. 54–75.

Driessler, H., 1932, *Die rheinische Mission in Südwestafrika*, Gutersloh.

Duffy, James, 1962, *Portugal in Africa*, Harmondsworth.

Duffy, James, 1967, *A question of slavery*, Oxford.
Duparquet, Charles, 1880 and 1881, 'Voyage en Cimbébasie', in *Les Missions Catholiques*, XII, pp. 367–370, 378–382, 404–407, 416–418, 426–430, and XIII, pp. 476–477, 484–486, 500–501, 514–515, 524–525, 538–539, 559–561, 568–571, 580–581, 606–610.
Duparquet, Charles, 1953, *Viagens na Cimbebásia* (ed. G. S. Dias), Luanda.
Estermann, Charles, 1939, 'Coutumes des Mbali du sud d'Angola', in *Africa*, XII, pp. 74–86.
Estermann, Charles, 1956–1961, *Etnografia do sudoeste de Angola*, Lisboa, 3 volumes.
Estermann, Charles, 1964, 'Les Bantous du sud-ouest de l'Angola', in *Anthropos*, LIX, pp. 20–74.
Estermann, Charles, 1976, *The ethnography of southwestern Angola, I, the non-Bantu peoples, the Ambo ethnic group* (ed. G. D. Gibson), New York and London.
Fauvet, Paul, 1977, 'Angola, when the cobra strikes', in *People's Power in Mozambique, Angola and Guinea-Bissau*, 7 and 8, June, pp. 44–50.
Felner, Alfredo de Albuquerque, 1940, *Angola, apontamentos sobre a colonisação dos planaltos e litoral do sul de Angola* (ed. G. S. Dias), Lisboa.
Forté, H., 1931, *Compagnie de Mossamédès, Sud-Angola, historique et situation actuelle de la société, rapport d'inspection*, Paris.
Galvão, Henrique, 1930, *Huíla, relatório de governo, 1929*, Vila Nova de Famalição.
Galvão, Henrique, c. 1944, *Outras terras, outras gentes, viagens na Africa portuguesa, 25,000 quilómetros em Angola*, Porto (also published Lisboa, n.d., 2 volumes).
Geraldes, Carlos Mello, and Fragateiro, Bernardo d'Oliveira, 1910, *Le caoutchouc dans les colonies portugaises*, Lisboa.
Gibbons, Alfred St Hill, 1904, *Africa from South to North through Marotseland*, London and New York, 2 volumes.
Gibson, Alan George Sumner, 1905, *Between Cape Town and Loanda, a record of two journeys in South West Africa*, London.
Giraúl, Visconde de (Joaquim Cardoso Botelho da Costa), 1910, *A cultura do algodão e da borracha na província de Angola*, Lisboa.
Giraúl, Visconde de (Joaquim Cardoso Botelho da Costa), 1912, *A escravatura em Mossamedes*, Lisboa (authorship according to *Grande Enciclopédia Portuguesa e Brasileira*, XII, pp. 409–410; no author on publication).
Gluckman, Max, 1968, *The economy of the central Barotse plain*, second edition, Manchester.
Gomes, Henrique de Barros, 1894, 'O commercio de Angola, II', in *Portugal em Africa*, 4, April, pp. 113–121.
Gorges, E. H. L., and de Jager, Matt., 1917, *Report on the conduct of the Ovakuanyama chief Mandume and on the military operations conducted against him in Ovamboland*, Cape Town (Union Government Publication no. 37 of 1917).
Great Britain, Foreign Office, 1919, *Angola, including Cabinda*, London.

Select bibliography

Guerreiro, Manuel Viegas, 1968, *Bochimanes !Khũ de Angola, estudo etnográfico*, Lisboa.
Guilmin, Henri, 1895, 'Dans le Mossamèdes, province d'Angola', in *Bulletin de la Société de Géographie Commerciale*, XVII, pp. 318–335.
Guimarães, Venáncio, 1923, *A situação de Angola, para a história do reinado de Norton, factos e depoimentos*, Lisboa.
Guimarães, Manuel Marques, and Paiva, Artur, 1942, *A indústria da pesca, realidade económica de Angola; relatório da missão de estudo organizada e patrocinada pela comissão reguladora do comércio de bacalhau e pelo grémio dos armazenistas de mercearia*, no place of publication.
Hahn, Hugo, 1867, 'Hugo Hahn's Reise von Otjimbingue zum Cunene, 1866', *Petermann's Mitteilungen*, XIII, pp. 284–298.
Hammond, Richard J., 1966, *Portugal and Africa, 1815–1910, a study in uneconomic imperialism*, Stanford.
Harms, Robert, 1975, 'The end of red rubber: a reassessment', *Journal of African History*, XVI, 1, pp. 73–88.
Hattingh, Johannes L., 1975, 'Die trekke uit die Suid-Afrikaanse Republieke en die Oranje-Vrystaat, 1875–1895', Ph.D. Thesis, University of Pretoria.
Hauenstein, Alfred, 1967, *Les Hanya*, Wiesbaden.
Heese, Hans F., 1976, 'Die Afrikaners in Angola, 1880–1928', Ph.D. Thesis, University of Cape Town.
Heimer, Franz-Wilhelm, 1972, *Educação e sociedade nas áreas rurais de Angola, resultados de um inquérito, Volume 1, apresentação do inquérito e estatísticas descritivas*, Luanda.
Heimer, Franz-Wilhelm, 1976, 'Décolonisation et légitimité politique en Angola', *Revue Française d'Etudes Politiques Africaines*, XI, 126, June, pp. 48–72.
Hindess, Barry, and Hirst, Paul Q., 1975, *Pre-capitalist modes of production*, London.
Hindess, Barry, and Hirst, Paul Q., 1977, *Mode of production and social formation, an auto-critique of pre-capitalist modes of production*, London.
Hobsbawm, Eric, 1969, *Bandits*, London.
Hobson, R. H., 1960, *Rubber, a footnote to Northern Rhodesian history*, Livingstone.
Holub, Emil, 1881, *Seven years in South Africa*, London, 2 volumes.
Iria, Alberto, 1942, *A colonização algarvia no sul de Angola*, Lagos.
Iria, Alberto, 1971, *Caíques do Algarve no sul de Angola*, Lisboa.
Katzenellenbogen, Simon E., 1973, *Railways and the copper mines of Katanga*, Oxford.
Keiling, Louis Alfred, 1934, *Quarenta anos de Africa*, Braga.
Kieran, J. A. P., 1966, 'The Holy Ghost Fathers in East Africa, 1863–1914', Ph.D. Thesis, University of London.
Kieran, J. A. P., 1969, 'Some Roman Catholic mission attitudes to Africans in nineteenth century East Africa', *Race*, X, 3, pp. 341–359.
Kuder, Manfred, 1971, *Angola, eine geographische, soziale und wirtschaftliche Landeskunde*, Darmstadt.

Lang, A., and Tastevin, C., 1937, *La tribu des Va-Nyaneka*, Corbeil (Mission Rohan-Chabot, Angola et Rhodesia, 1912–1914, Tome V, Ethnographie).

Lebzelter, Victor, 1934, *Eingeborenenkulturen in Südwest und Südafrika*, Leipzig.

Lehmann, F. Rudolph, 1954, 'Die anthropogeographischen Verhältnisse des Ambolandes im nördlichen Südwestafrika', in *Zeitschrift für Ethnologie*, LXXIX, pp. 8–58.

Lehmann, F. Rudolph, 1954–1955, 'Die politische und soziale Stellung der Häuptlinge im Ovamboland während der deutschen Schutzherrschaft in Südwestafrika', in *Tribus*, new series, IV–V, pp. 265–328.

Leutwein, Theodor Gotthilf von, 1907, *Elf Jahre Gouverneur in Deutsch-Südwestafrika*, Berlin, second edition.

Lima, Bernardo Vellez de, 1911, *O districto de Mossamedes, assumptos locaes, carta aberta ao illustre deputado pelo círculo . . .*, Castello de Vide.

Lima, Maria Helena Figueiredo, 1977, *Nação Ovambo*, Lisboa.

Livingstone, David, 1959, *Livingstone's family letters, 1841–1856* (ed. I. Schapera), London, 2 volumes.

Livingstone, David, 1963, *Livingstone's African Journals, 1853–1856* (ed. I. Schapera), London, 2 volumes.

Loeb, Edwin M., 1962, *In feudal Africa*, published as Part II, XXVIII, 3, July, of *International Journal of American Linguistics*, Bloomington.

Lopo, Júlio de Castro, 1964, *Jornalismo de Angola, subsídios para a sua história*, Luanda.

McCulloch, Meran, 1951, *The southern Lunda and related peoples*, London.

Machado, Carlos Roma, 1918, 'Colonização do planalto de Huila e Mossamedes', in *Boletim da Sociedade de Geografia de Lisboa*, XXXVI, pp. 267–309.

Machado, Ernesto, 1956, *No sul de Angola*, Lisboa.

McKiernan, Gerald, 1954, *The narrative and journal of Gerald McKiernan in South West Africa* (ed. P. Serton), Cape Town.

Magyar, Ladislas, 1859, *Reisen in Süd-Afrika in den Jahren 1849 bis 1857*, Leipzig and Pest.

Mainga, Mutumba, 1973, *Bulozi under the Luyana kings*, London.

Marques, Walter, 1964–1965, *Problemas do desenvolvimento económico de Angola*, Luanda, 2 volumes.

Marques, A. H. de Oliveira, 1973, *História de Portugal, Volume II, das revoluções liberais aos nossos dias*, Lisboa.

Marvaud, Angel, 1912, *Le Portugal et ses colonies*, Paris.

Matos, José Ribeiro Norton de, 1926, *A província de Angola*, Porto.

Matta, Sebastião Nunes da, 1867, 'Relatório, 7/2/1867', in *Boletim Oficial*, suplemento ao numero 24, 17/6/1867.

Medeiros, Carlos Alberto, 1976, *A colonização das terras altas da Huíla (Angola), estudo de geografia humana*, Lisboa.

Mendes, Afonso, 1958, *A Huíla e Moçâmedes, considerações sobre o trabalho indígena*, Lisboa.

Menezes, Sebastião Lopes de Calheiros e, 1867, *Relatório do governador geral da província de Angola, referido ao anno de 1861*, Lisboa.

Meyer, Hans, 1918, *Das portugiesische Kolonialreich der Gegenwart*, Berlin.

Milheiros, Mário, 1972, *Indice histórico-corográfico de Angola*, Luanda.

Miller, Joseph, 1970, 'Cokwe trade and conquest in the nineteenth century', in R. Gray and D. Birmingham (eds.), *Pre-colonial African trade*, London, pp. 175–201.

Miller, Joseph, 1973, 'Requiem for the Jaga', in *Cahiers d'Etudes Africaines*, XIII, 49, pp. 120–149.

Möller, Peter August, 1974, *Journey into Africa through Angola, Ovampoland and Damaraland, 1895–1896* (ed. and tr. by I. and J. Rudner), Cape Town.

Monteiro, Joaquim John, 1968, *Angola and the river Congo*, London, 2 volumes, reprint of 1875 edition.

Moorsom, Richard, 1973 'Colonisation and proletarianisation: an exploratory investigation of the formation of the working class in Namibia under German and South African colonial rule to 1945', M.A. Thesis, University of Sussex.

Moorsom, Richard, 1977, 'Underdevelopment, contract labour and worker consciousness in Namibia, 1915–1972', *Journal of Southern African Studies*, IV, 1, October, pp. 52–87.

Munro, J. Forbes, 1976, *Africa and the international economy, 1800–1960*, London.

Nascimento, José Pereira do, 1891, *Da Huíla às terras do Humbe, notas a lápis*, Huíla.

Nascimento, José Pereira do, 1892, *O districto de Mossamedes*, Lisboa.

Nascimento, José Pereira do, 1894, 'Missões de Benguela', in *Portugal em Africa*, 1, January, pp. 17–21.

Nascimento, José Pereira do, 1898, *Exploração geográfica e mineral no districto de Mossamedes em 1894–1895*, Lisboa (also published as annex to *Portugal em Africa*, 1898).

Nascimento, Ruy, and Silva, F. Marques, 1959, *Notas sobre as indústrias de transformação do pescado em Angola*, Lisboa.

Negreiros, A. de Almada, 1907, *Les colonies portugaises*, Paris.

Neto, José Pereira, 1963, *O Baixo Cunene, subsídios para o seu desenvolvimento*, Lisboa.

Nitsche, Georg, 1913, *Ovamboland, Versuch einer landeskundlichen Darstellung nach dem gegenwärtigen Stand unser geographischen Kenntnis*, Kiel.

Nogueira, António Francisco, 1880, *A raça negra, sob o ponto de visto da civilisação da Africa*, Lisboa.

Oliveira, Mário António Fernandes de, 1968–1971, *Angolana, documentação sobre Angola*, Lisbon and Luanda, 2 volumes.

Paiva, Artur de, 1938, *Artur de Paiva* (ed. G. S. Dias), Lisbon, 2 volumes.

Palgrave, William Coates, 1969, *Report of Mr. Palgrave, special commissioner, of his mission to Damaraland and Great Namaqualand in 1876*, Pretoria, reprint of 1877 edition.

Papagno, Giuseppe, 1972, *Colonialismo e feudalesimo, la questione dei prazos da coroa nel Mozambico alla fine del secolo XIX*, Torino.

Pearson, Emil, 1970, *Ngangela–English dictionary*, Cuernavaca.

Pélissier, René, 1975, 'Résistance et révoltes en Angola, 1845–1961', Thèse d'Etat, Académie de Paris, 3 volumes. (Published Orgeval, 1977–8.)

Perrings, Charles, 1977, 'Good lawyers but poor workers, recruited Angolan labourers in the copper mines of Katanga, 1917–1921', *Journal of African History*, XVIII, 2, pp. 237–259.

Pimentel, Fernando, 1903, *Investigação commercial na província de Angola em 1902–1903*, Porto.

Pinto, Alexandre Serpa, 1881, *Como eu atravessei Africa*, London, 2 volumes (also published in English edition).

Portugal, Governo Português, 1903, *Questão do Barotze, memória do governo português para recurso á arbitragem de Sua Majestade o rei de Itália*, Lisboa.

Portugal, Ministério da Marinha e do Ultramar, 1897, *A questão da borracha em Angola, documentos officiaes, primeira serie*, Lisboa.

Portugal, Ministério das Colónias, 1912, *Estatística dos caminhos de ferro das colónias portuguesas de 1888 a 1910*, Lisboa.

Portgual, Ministério das Colónias, 1918, *Relatórios e informações, 5, Inquérito sobre a produção do trigo nos planaltos de Benguela e Huíla, 1917*, pp. 357–481, Coimbra.

Pössinger, Hermann, 1973, 'Interrelations between economic and social change in rural Africa, the case of the Ovimbundu of Angola', in F. W. Heimer (ed.), *Social change in Angola*, München, pp. 32–52.

Postma, Dirk, 1897, *De trekboeren te St. Januario Humpata*, Amsterdam and Pretoria.

Rates, J. Carlos, 1929, *Angola, Moçambique, São Tomé*, Lisboa.

Roçadas, José Augusto Alves, 1908, *O sul de Angola*, Lisboa.

Roçadas, José Augusto Alves, 1914, *La main d'oeuvre indigène à Angola*, Lisboa.

Roçadas, José Augusto Alves, 1919, *Relatório sobre as operações no sul de Angola em 1914*, Lisboa.

Rogado, Quintino, 1957, *O tenente Quintino Rogado* (ed. G. S. Dias), Lisboa (Agência Geral das Colónias, Coleção Pelo Império, 127).

Samuels, Michael Anthony, 1970, *Education in Angola, 1878–1914*, New York.

Santos, Afonso Costa Valdez Thomaz dos, 1945, *Angola, coração do império*, Lisboa.

Santos, Ignácio, 1898, 'A missão do Jau' and 'Modo de viver dos pretos no planalto de Mossamedes', *Portugal em Africa*, 58–60, October to December, pp. 400–404, 450–454 and 495–502.

Sarmento, Alexandre, 1945, *O negro de Menongue, notas antropológicas e etnográficas*, Lisboa.

Schachtzabel, Alfred, 1923, *Im Hochland von Angola*, Dresden.

Schinz, Hans, 1891, *Deutsch-Südwest-Afrika, forschungreisen durch die deutschen Schutzgebiete Gross-Nama- und Hereroland nach dem Kunene, dem Ngami-See und der Kalahari, 1884–1887*, Oldenburg.

Schlettwein, C., 1907, *Der Farmer in Deutsch-Südwest-Afrika*, Wismar.

Seiner, Franz, 1909, *Ergebnisse einer Bereisung des Gebiets zwischen Okawango und Sambesi (Caprivi-Zipfel) in den Jahren 1905 und 1906*, Berlin.

Sideri, S., 1970, *Trade and power, informal colonialism in Anglo-Portuguese relations*, Rotterdam.

Silva, Raúl José Candeias da, 1971–1973, 'Subsídios para a história da colonização do distrito de Moçâmedes durante o século XIX', *Studia*, 32, pp. 371–378, 33, pp. 341–372, 34, pp. 481–534, 35, pp. 421–439, 36, pp. 293–390.

Silva, Elisete Marques da, 1978, 'O impacto da dominação colonial nas sociedades africanas do sul de Angola', forthcoming in *The formation of Angolan society*, F. W. Heimer (ed.), London.

Sousa, Rodolpho de Santa Brigida de, 1887, 'Mossamedes', *Boletim da Sociedade de Geografia de Lisboa*, VII, 6, pp. 396–414.

Stals, E. L. P., 1968, 'Die aanraking tussen Blankes en Ovambo's in Suidwes-Afrika, 1850–1915', *Archives Year Book for South African History*, XXXI, 2, pp. 219–349.

Statham, John C. B., 1922, *Through Angola, a coming colony*, Edinburgh.

Stevenson-Hamilton, James, 1953, *The Barotseland journal of James Stevenson-Hamilton, 1898–1899* (ed. J. P. R. Wallis), London.

Tabler, Edward C., 1973, *Pioneers of South West Africa and Ngamiland, 1738–1880*, Cape Town.

Tams, G., 1969, *Visit to the Portuguese possessions in south-western Africa*, New York, 2 volumes, translated from German edition of 1845.

Teixeira, Alberto de Almeida, 1934, *Angola intangível*, Porto.

Tönjes, Hermann, 1911, *Ovamboland, Land, Leute, Mission, mit besonderer Berücksichtung seines grössten Stammes Oukuanjama*, Berlin.

Torres, Manuel de Mendonça, 1950, *O distrito de Moçâmedes nas fases da origem e da primeira organização, 1485–1859*, Lisboa.

Torres, Manuel de Mendonça, 1952, 'A cultura do algodoeiro no distrito de Moçâmedes durante a guerra civil americana e no período da reconstrução', *Boletim Geral do Ultramar*, 328, pp. 15–58.

Urquhart, Alvin W., 1963, *Patterns of settlement and subsistence in southwestern Angola*, Washington.

Van der Merwe, P. J., 1951, *Ons halfeeu in Angola, 1880–1928*, Johannesburg.

Van Warmelo, N. J., 1951, *Notes on the Kaokoveld (South West Africa) and its peoples*, Pretoria.

Vellut, Jean-Luc, 1977, 'Rural poverty in western Shaba, c. 1890–1930', *The roots of rural poverty in central and southern Africa*, R. Palmer and Q. N. Parsons (eds.), London, pp. 294–316.

Vidal, João Evangelista Lima, 1912, *Visitas Pastoraes em 1910*, Luanda (Diocese de Angola e Congo).

Vilela, Afonso José, 1923, *A pesca e indústrias derivadas no distrito de Mossamedes, 1921–1922*, Porto.

Viúva Bastos e Filhos, 1913, *A derrocada, carta aberta ao Senhor Ministro das Colónias*, Lisboa.

Wellington, John Harold, 1967, *South West Africa and its human issues*, Oxford.

Wheeler, Douglas L., 1967, *Portuguese expansion in Angola since 1836, a re-examination*, Salisbury (Central Africa Historical Association, local series, pamphlet 20).

Wheeler, Douglas L., and Pélissier, René, 1971, *Angola*, London.

White, Arthur Silva, 1892, *The development of Africa; a study in applied geography*, London, second edition.

Wieder, Padre, 1892, 'O Jau', in *Boletim da Sociedade de Geografia de Lisboa*, XI, 10, pp. 711–729.

Wilson, Monica, and Thompson, Leonard (eds.), 1971, *The Oxford history of South Africa*, Volume II, Oxford.

Wolpe, Harold, 1974, 'The theory of internal colonization, the South African case', *The Societies of Southern Africa in the 19th and 20th Centuries*, IV, pp. 105–120.

Index

128